Say "Yes" to Love
God Leads Humanity Toward Christ Consciousness

Through
Yaël and Doug Powell

Circle of Light Press
Eureka Springs, Arkansas

Say 'Yes' To Love,
God Leads Humanity Toward Christ Consciousness
Through Yaël and Doug Powell

Copyright ©2003 by Yaël and Doug Powell

Paperback Original ISBN 0-9725991-3-4
Circle of Light Press

Yaël and Doug Powell
Circle of Light
3969 Mundell Road
Eureka Springs, AR 72631

Cover illustration and book layout by Judith Bicking
Compilation, editing of Messages by Shanna Mac Lean

web site: www.circleoflight.net
email: connect@circleoflight.net

Printing: InstantPublisher.com Collierville, TN

SAY 'YES' TO LOVE SERIES
Through Yaël and Doug Powell
Circle of Light Press

Say "Yes" to Love, God Explains SoulMates

*Say "Yes" to Love, God Unveils
SoulMate Love and Sacred Sexuality*

Say "Yes" to Love, God's Guidance to LightWorkers

*Say "Yes" to Love, God Leads Humanity
Toward Christ Consciousness*

Soon to be published

Say "Yes" to Love, Giving Birth to the Christ Light

WORDS FROM OUR READERS

"I proceed very slowly reading these Messages because it's as if it weren't my eyes that were reading it, but my heart. It's as if I've just come Home. Your Messages are so "soft." I don't know how else to describe them. It feels like being wrapped in something very delicate. I keep crying all the time when I read them... I feel so very beloved." Paula Launonen, Ravenna, Italy

"Reading the Messages from God is like communing with God. Even if they are addressed to all humanity, they can also be a very personal experience. When you read the Messages from God, your heart will open and stay open if you so choose. A cascade of sparkling, fresh, flowing, colored Love energy. In Love from Love to Love creating more Love. I will be thankful forever." Tiziana Paggiolu, London, England

"Everything in the Messages resonates so deeply in me. I am amazed that I've found so much that had already been revealed to me in visions and dreams...it sometimes takes my breath away! It has given so much validity to everything I had already come to believe. Thank you all for feeling the need to share the Messages. They have meant so much to me in my journey. It's kind of like piloting a boat by the stars and one day discovering a secret compartment full of maps that show where all the ports of call are located. It makes it so much easier to get where you want to go!" Diane Dunville, Lanexa, VA

"These messages are an incredible blessing — a flow of Love so beautiful, so clear; so full of truth and understanding that they are like a drink from a mountain stream! These messages are this to me, and so much more. These messages are the road home!" Robert Austin-Murphy, Bellingham, WA

"Words are so inadequate to describe how these books have touched my life... It's what I always thought relationships can be, and I never found it put into black and white. Here it was, so perfectly described.

I devoured it like I would the finest 'crème brulé', not stopping until I had every last morsel of it, and then craved for more. It came at a time when I had said to my friends, "I found my Twin Flame, never knowing what it meant. Now I know." Carol Davis, Cat Spring, Texas

"In all my study, discernment, and spiritual practice over the years, I found that each teaching was only a step, only part of the process. I have known that each of us is so much more than our limited experiences have shown us. I seemed to need the bigger picture. I began to believe that I just was not ready or open enough to receive this divine manifestation. Then came "Say 'YES' to Love." That grace, that grandness, that confirmation that we are so much more than we can ever imagine sang out to me boldly. The whole of co-creation was simplified and resonated fully within me. The consistent theme is that we are truly only Love and are much more than we can now comprehend. "Say 'YES' to Love" is also very practical — most notably in how to function in a world of duality when you know only Love is real. Just as the pressure of others' duality began eroding my knowing, this book arrived to help gently guide me. Just as Creator promised." Peggy Zetler, Dillon, Montana.

"These Messages are stunning, clear, beautiful, re-activating, stirring to the core of my being. This material reminds me of Home, reminds me to express the totality of my being, reminds me of how close to Home we are now, reminds me of my Twin Flame. Just having the books and knowing their content is a small sign of the ecstasy to come." Karen Porrit, U.K.

"These Messages, faithfully documented by Yaël Powell, were brought to me at just the right time in my life and served as validation of what my Twin Flame and I had discovered on our own, without any outside influence. I can speak personally on the validity of this Twin Flame relationship as I was blessed enough in my lifetime to have been with my Twin Flame. Our story is for another time and another place, but it is important to state without qualification that the reality of the soulmate bond as expressed through God's Messages is not a fabrication or an idealistic view of what love can be... It is the greatest love that can be, the love of our Creator to us, and the ability to experience that kind of love within our soulmate bond." Rev. Adelle Tilton, The Church of Interfaith Christians, NE

DEDICATION

This book is dedicated to Jesus —
heart of the heart of God,
center of the center —
who came to Earth in all of
his pristine beauty and took upon
himself the pain of our
separation from God, that he might
be a bridge for us.
He is the bridge by which we
go back Home.
Invite him in as you read these
Messages from God,
and he will help you —
not only to understand, but to
live Christ Consciousness.

SAY 'YES' TO LOVE,
GOD LEADS HUMANITY
TOWARD CHRIST CONSCIOUSNESS

TABLE OF CONTENTS

THE MESSAGES FROM GOD

Christ Consciousness 15

Praying Gratitude 27

The Next Step: Co-Creation
Through Praying Gratitude 41

Abundance and Co-Creation.
The Principles and the Steps 57

Abundance. Living the Will of God 73

Abundance. The Pattern 85

Abundance. The Bridge of Gratitude 97

Abundance. God's Garden Is Our Consciousness 111

Becoming the Will of God. Seeing as God Sees 127

Becoming the River of Love.
The Ascension Happens Naturally 139

Moving into the New World Now 151

Our Heart's Desire 163

Making the Leap. Becoming Only Love
as We Give Our Will to God 175

Experiencing Ourselves as in God.
Remembrance of Being God's Heart 189

If God is Love and This World is Not,
Then Obviously This World Is Not Real.
Making the Choice 203

Love Me Until Only I Am Real
and You Will Have All Your Answers 213

The Emotion of Divine Love is the
Only True Power in All Creation 227

TO MY FATHER

I would like to thank my father, who took me to the pits of hell that I might anchor the light there and that I might have such deep compassion for all who share this journey of life on Earth. May I see how every episode of rape, abuse and cruelty served me well in my resolve to find a different way to live. May I grow daily in this gratitude to him! May I love him with God's pure, unwavering Love. May I know with everything I Am that there is nothing to forgive, for there is truly only Love. Ury, wherever you are, may you be free as well from any beliefs about the roles we played. Thank you for showing me the darkness that I could understand my dedication to the light.

ACKNOWLEDGEMENTS

I first acknowledge my beloved Doug, my SoulMate, whom I love more deeply every day. Doug's increasing light and clarity is a continual inspiration to me and to all who know him. We have truly walked every step of this path together, from being two individuals full of fear and ego, to recognizing our SoulMate relationship and claiming daily more of the passion, beauty and ecstasy that God keeps lovingly showing us. I am so deeply grateful to God for tenderly unveiling to me my magnificent SoulMate, Doug.

Next to Doug, Shanna is my truest Soul Family. Shanna has not only catalyzed these books into print. She has held up a divine mirror of pure Love and shown me my true self. Thanks to her I have finally completely accepted the gift of bringing forth these Messages. I have moved beyond the fear of ego that kept me hidden, afraid to come forth, lest I "think too much of myself." Through Shanna's Love, I came to see myself with enough clarity that God could show me how the "trickster" ego can use even "humility" to keep us from totally giving our lives in service! Shanna is the most pure, light-filled being I have ever met. That God brought her "miraculously" into our lives in order to bring forth these Messages is one of our greatest gifts. Until Shanna I have never before known anyone whose life, dedication and Love of God so closely reflected my own. Though God is the author of these Messages, it is

Shanna's hands that have shaped them into books.

I thank our sweet Mary, whose life belongs totally to God, for typing these Messages and blessing them with her Love. May she ever be a part of the Team, being grown and nourished as we are by these Messages. I acknowledge her SoulMate, Steve, and her son, Michael, a young man who was raised completely conscious of spiritual reality. He is amazing!

I deeply thank Suzanne Muller, the woman who saved my life by taking me from the absolute terror of a life filled with sexual and physical abuse and darkness. Suzanne placed my feet upon the Path of Light by teaching me to meditate thirty years ago, thus establishing in my life the spiritual practice which has ultimately brought forth these Messages.

And to my beloved friend, Susan Lee Solar, wherever you are beyond the veil, thank you, thank you for all the ways you brought life back to me. Your spirit of adventure, your deep connection to the seasons of the Earth, the cats, the laughter and your part in bringing Doug and me together. I know that your adventures continue and that all who are near you are blessed.

To everyone who has touched my life, I give thanks!

Yaël

INTRODUCTION

How can I tell you what it means to be the instrument through which these Messages have come? I am "the pen in God's hand," but I am also the feet upon the path. From the moment these Messages began in earnest when my husband, Doug, and I came together until now, every day I have been tenderly loved and patiently grown. Through the most personal, amazing and gentle Love, God has taken us from being two people filled with fear and pain, afraid of Love, to a glorious experience of joy together in which every day is a miracle.

Out of all that I have learned, all the glistening moments of transcendence, the experiences of awakening and of daily transformation, the greatest of all is the knowledge and experience of God's Love. It is so personal. It is sweet, tender, and completely unconditional. It is an experience of being bathed in reassurance, yet being lifted each moment into a grand perspective of every detail of life. God answers every question! This has been a continual amazement to me. And this glorious yet personal, vast but intimately present relationship with God is there for each of us. Its acceptance is the key to it all.

God has taken my heart and opened it, step by patient step. With each step God became more personal, not less. How can I describe it? It is an expansion into the great magnificence, the glory of Creation, the ecstasy of ever touching more of the wholeness that is God. Yet with each and every expansion of my heart, God's tender Love was ever more connected with my life, and more and more a part of my experience of each moment.

How God can be the great Creator, so vast our minds can't gasp it, and at the same time be so intimately present, so personal and so tender is our greatest gift. It is a mystery to our minds, but as you read these Messages, your heart will know its truth—the truth that each of us is loved perfectly and personally by God. This is why I've used this word "personal" from the moment this experience began in 1986. No other word could describe this sweet communion or explain the seeming mystery of this great Love.

At first I was resistant to sharing these Messages because my experience of this communion was so deep, so close, so personal that every nuance of my life was exposed as God led me beyond the world of ego. My ego, ever tricky, also said I was not worthy. "How could anyone be clear enough to be the instrument to receive Messages from God," it said, "let alone you!"

Then in the spring of 2000 I had a near-death experience. I went through what God called the "living bardo." I confronted every fear I'd ever had, and I discovered that I still withheld a little piece of my heart from God. I found I'd kept a little wedge between us. I saw that I still blamed God for my son's death, and that I still harbored shreds of doubt since "God had not been there for me," through all the pain and incest of my childhood. At last I fully gave my heart. I gave my life. I gave my Will to God completely. I closed that little gap where I held my little Will. Immediately I knew that I would live.

At that moment everything changed. What had been a "journey" of daily steps assisted each day through God's Messages became a living transformation. My heart cracked open and Love became my life, and the Messages and experiences that are in this book began. This book is an arc, a trajectory, that has completely changed everything I thought I knew about life, about this world and about that which we call Christ consciousness.

Beginning with the book, *Say "Yes" to Love, God's Guidance to LightWorkers* and going on through many books beyond this one, these Messages create a bridge that God is building across which all of humanity will travel. It is a bridge of consciousness that takes us from our life in the world to our life in God. As we cross this bridge, we move from a world of duality – of light and dark, pleasure and pain, good and evil — to a world of unity in which there is only Love.

As these Messages were given, we at Circle of Light were crossing this bridge ourselves, walking every step, asking every question, making every shift. Some of the Messages were answers to our questions. Others were streams of Love rushing through me outward to humanity. All were an experience of being lifted in such tenderness, such personal and uplifting Love that each Message has been a life-changing experience.

This Love will enfold you, too, as you read, for beneath the words and concepts are packages of Love being carried right to you to verify the content of these Messages and to bring you, too, into an ever-deeper personal relationship with God. God, the wonder-filled magnificence, while beyond our mental comprehension, is completely accessible through our hearts. You will discover, as we have, that it is within our very hearts that this bridge is being constructed.

Sitting in meditation seven years ago, God first revealed to me what I termed the "New World." It came about after a long conversation with a member of Greenpeace. She had carefully shown us proof after proof that this world is well beyond the hope of saving. The pollution is too high. The population is multiplying until soon the very numbers will prove impossible for the Earth to sustain. In deep distress after hearing this, I turned to God and asked if this were true. Were we here on a dying planet? Was it too late?

In answer I was lifted into a different view, another experience – that of an Earth of joy and glorious, rich abundance. I felt the peace. I shared a world of pristine hues and beauty in which there was communion between every form of life. Then, God clearly said: "There is a New World. But, you can't get there from here." Now I have more fully experienced this New World. It is not a place. It is a shift in consciousness. In God's presence, as I sit each day in meditation, the New World becomes ever clearer and the Old World fades away.

If your hands are on this book, you are ready, and nothing you believe about your life can keep you from traversing this bridge. Your heart now becomes your perception of the world, its reality affirmed as you read. You also are a bridge for all others who are drawn into your life. And so we build it, heart by heart, turning to God for understanding the steps, then giving the Love we are given.

It is not too late for our precious Earth, nor will there be any "left behind." Instead, we are all in the midst of a miracle, part of which is recorded in these pages.

I "live my life" in a body filled with pain. I am often in bed, mostly "housebound," yet I spend my moments in bliss, surrounded by beauty, in ecstatic Love with my SoulMate. I share this simply as a way of telling you that no situation or circumstance can affect a waking heart or restrict you in any way from saying "Yes" to Love. Then, as we've "bridged the gap" between every human heart here on Earth, every last experience of negativity will fade as all life on Earth comes back to Love.

God's covenant with us is this. Everything we believe with all our heart, God will help us create, for we are co-creators with God. Until now our heart's beliefs have been those of suffering and pain. These Messages from God are here to change this and to lead each one of us back to Love. This means Love on every level – the presence of our SoulMate beside us in this life (see *Say "Yes" to Love, God Explains SoulMates* for more on this) and the presence of our heart's belief in only Love, which will bring forth the world of which we dream. It is a world of peace and plenty. It is a world of unity – a world where each person shares everything he or she has so that every human being has everything he or she wants. It is a whole where every impulse is to unify. And it is a world of such magnificence and beauty that each moment is a treasure beyond describing. That world is waiting for us, and these Messages from God are the bridge to get us there.

Yaël
Circle of Light
April 2003

A NOTE FROM THE EDITOR

I met Yaël and Doug Powell on July 17th, 2001.
God led me right to them through a series of synchronous
events. Because of her disability, Yaël rarely leaves her
home but she and Doug had decided very spontaneously
to celebrate her birthday at the home of a close friend in
Fayetteville, one hour away. That friend had also
graciously agreed to host me, a complete stranger, for a
few days, while I explored the Fayetteville, AR area. When
I arrived at her door, Yaël greeted me.

As I sat with Yaël and Doug that evening, I was
fascinated by their obvious living Love for each other, a
Love that pervaded their every word and movement. I
learned about Yaël's constant pain from a genetic disease
of the spine that severely limits her movement, and
about Circle of Light, their spiritual center in Eureka
Springs. Following dinner Yaël read one of the "Messages
from God" that have come through her during thirty
years of daily meditation. I felt indescribable excitement
and upliftment from the extraordinary vibration created
and the amazing information of this Message.

We quickly recognized ourselves as the ancient
soul family we are, and spent two bliss filled days
together at Circle of Light, reconnecting, sharing our
lives and our spiritual journeys. Our coming together
was divinely guided, step-by-step. Yaël and Doug showed
me (then) fifty hand-written notebooks of Messages

from God! I committed myself on the spot to utilizing my writing, editing and organizational skills to help them bring this illuminated and needed material out into the world. Our first joint publication effort, *Say "Yes" to Love, God Explains SoulMates,* was accomplished from a distance, and just before Christmas 2001 I took up residence in my new home at Circle of Light Spiritual Center.

After my arrival our "training" began in earnest. The daily Messages intensified, many with specific personal directives for each of us. We all experienced a series of great shifts in consciousness that are ongoing. Within a few months we had the entire content of two more books in the *Say "Yes" to Love* series, *God Unveils SoulMate Love and Sacred Sexuality,* as well as *God's Guidance to LightWorkers.* During the last several months our inner training has been directed to what God has called "approaching and accepting Christ consciousness." As quickly as we absorb what is being taught, the material is edited to be outgoing to humanity. With humility and honor, we accept our roles as conduits. Thus, the fourth book in the *Say "Yes" series, God Leads Humanity Toward Christ Consciousness* is now in your hands and its companion, *Giving Birth to the Christ Light*, will soon follow.

Life at Circle of Light is a series of miracles. The natural beauty of the lake, mountains and surrounding woods creates a vibration of the New World. The evening sunsets are otherworldly. We watch in awe. Every day Yaël meditates several hours, bringing through the amazing teachings from God. The highlight of each day is reading the new Message together. I assist in managing our active wedding business, compiling and editing Messages, directing the growing communication from our website, www.circleoflight.net, helping with practical life necessities and tending the organic garden. I have the joyous feeling of knowing I am in the right place at the right time, with my soul family, doing the tasks for which I have long been prepared. I have never been happier! Our commitment as a spiritual family is to bring God's Message of Love forth to our brothers and sisters.

Shanna Mac Lean
Eureka Springs
April 2003

The Messages
From God

As you become Christed beings,
all you will see is
the most tender Love.
All you will feel is
the joyous privilege of being able
to touch one more piece of
Our great being.

Christ Consciousness

Christ consciousness. What does this mean – these words that represent the goal to many of you? You are here now at the gate, the doorway, wondering how to get in. Many of you have been asking Me questions – good questions that together we will answer for others also coming this way.

You have believed that this consciousness was to be born within, and that you would come to hear My voice as the "still small voice" within you. You have attempted to find this communion somehow "inside" of you, believing that "looking up" to Me certainly could not be Christ consciousness. Everything you have ever read has presented this as an inner victory, an inner experience of transformation, a connection bringing Me forth in a personal way.

However, I have given you many experiences. I have taken you out of your smaller selves. I have shown you that I Am All, All in All in All, and that I cradle you tenderly in an expanding Love that goes forth, all around you forever.

How do you relate this to being here, to choosing to be "Christ consciousness"?

I am taking you careful step by careful step, until the seed of understanding sprouts within, and you become the growing plant. The intellect cannot feed you. It is like trying to hold water in a sieve. The intellect has no real substance, no structure with which to hold the truth. So I use it sparingly – only enough to engage the heart, for that is the only way to understanding.

Now I will begin to answer your questions. Why now, when some of you have been asking for some time? Because all of you together have been growing into this. As each of you understands another part, you build an awareness, the "space" in your heart, even if you do not voice your understandings. So will it be with all of humanity, as choice-by-choice and awakening-by-awakening, a new consciousness is woven together, linking the cells of My heart to each other.

You have no boundaries. The Love that I Am is you. Let Me say this to you again. You have no boundaries. The Love that I Am is you. Think upon this. Allow this thought to open you to all the possibilities of that statement.

If you have no boundaries… if the truth of your being is Love, then I could not condone a belief that Christ consciousness is something that happens within you, within this little human being, this package pretending to be the whole thing. This would be a consciousness of limitation. Even if you see Christ consciousness as the highest attainment you will ever reach, seeing it as within this you, this human self, is like thinking the ocean is one tiny tide pool.

Therefore, I propose to you that Christ consciousness is that shift in what you see as the background and what you see in your foreground of your life. Beloved ones, you will know you are near when there is no one there to "know" with!

Yes, Jesus is your example — but not the Jesus of historical pages, whose words have been translated through human minds (though even so they have kept their vibrational truth, of course). No, I propose that you become students of the living Jesus, the one who IS the light to lead all humanity through this change.

Oh, but I will show you also! If you have a personal communion with Me, then there is nowhere else you need to go. Nothing else you need to learn. Here is the "knob on the doorway," dear ones. *Surrender into Love. Surrender into Love for Me. That IS Christ consciousness! For what is Christ? My living Love. What are you? Love's vehicle.*

You are My heart, beloved ones. This I tell you constantly. Well, what is the purpose of a heart, spiritually? To pour forth Love. This then is the answer you seek. This is who you are. This is your Homecoming. Your awakening. Oh, is it not obvious? If you are My heart, then everything you are is centered in My Love, holding My Love and sending it forth, for that is the function of a heart on every level. Love is the very substance of life. It is the lifeblood of Creation.

So, just as your physical heart pumps blood to nourish the physical vehicle, so must the spiritual heart "pump" Love. If your physical heart stops being a vehicle for lifeblood, the body cannot survive. Beloveds, just so if you who are the heart of God stop pouring forth My Love, you become "dead" spiritually. No matter what you may ever tell yourself. No matter how many lifetimes of "personal growth." No matter how much "good" you believe you do, *you will not truly be alive spiritually until you reclaim your position as My heart.*

I can tell you there are very few who ever get anywhere close to this doorway — this true question about Christ consciousness. Even you who are spiritually "awake" and asking questions have only now gotten there! This shows you that it is not easy from here, in this world around you, within "the illusion."* But, of course, that is what we now change, by clearly marking the pathway Home, so that for others it will be far less intense.

Only recently have some of you truly longed to feel divine Love. To give divine Love. My Love. Not human love. And even though you knew you had never felt it, you wanted it. This is the key. Truly I do wait on you, "knocking until you answer." And of course, beloveds, your answer grows, as we grow in our relationship. With every effort, your heart grows closer to remembering itself as the glorious cosmic vessel of Love.

Christ consciousness is the full experience that you are only and forever vehicles of divine Love. Once you fully grasp this, precious ones, you will be as

Jesus was. *Jesus had no boundaries. He did not see himself as a human being, even when expressing thus. He saw himself only and ever as a vessel of My Love.* His entire being was surrendered to this Love expressing through him. As you will discover, dear ones, the Love "within" him as Jesus and the Love all around him as Me were not separate. In every moment, he reached upward into Me, into the "universal" and brought divine Love through. And on its way through, it showed him his own truth and was all.

In this Love, he knew all things. In this Love, of course, he was (is) one with Me. *This Love became his complete and total identity.* There was nothing separate. No "Jesus," the man. Only Love given. And given. And given. And in the giving, of course, he received everything, for Love is what I Am. In pouring forth Love, Jesus knew himself. He knew Me. He knew all Creation, and all Creation knew him. As Love meeting and greeting Love, he could say to the elements "be still." Not as a command but because he knew himself in them (for, of course, they too are Love, even if influenced by humanity). So in loving communion, knowing his presence within All That Is, he was still and so were they.

Christ consciousness is, then, just this – the complete experience of yourself as the vessel and the vehicle for giving forth divine Love. Once you have fully experienced this, everything will be completely clear. There will be no more questions about where you fit or how you serve or about your relationship to anything and everything.

Then truly you will have "made the shift." There will be no "little self," at all. There is only Love. Thus, when you speak, it will be Love speaking – as it was through Jesus. This is why he said "I Am" with authority, because he truly was My vehicle, the heart through which I love. This is you also.

So there will be no "still small voice" within you. No! There will only be the living Love. It will pour through you like a rushing river of life, nourishing perfectly everything it touches, for Love is the lifeblood of Creation, the substance of which everything is made. *So when you are only the giving forth of Love, the "pumping heart of God," then any who come into contact will be nourished, fed.* Everything and everyone. Anyone in the proximity of such Love cannot but be affected. However, if they recognize themselves in it, then they will make a shift. To whatever degree they can accept it, to that degree will they be made whole.

I have said to you before that *to be Christed is to know only Love.*** Yet, as in all things, you are continually growing in your understanding of what I give. To be Christed is to know ONLY Love. Dear ones, you as your ego will disappear. Yes. Disappear. This is why the egos of humanity are fighting so valiantly. It is also why all of you must go forth with this truth. This is the very same "good news" of which Jesus spoke. Yet now it is meant at last for "the masses," for all of humanity.

Truly as you grow into Christ consciousness, you will love them all equally, beloved ones, you who serve

Me. ***You will love them equally and passionately because you will be nothing else so you will see nothing else.*** You will look at any and every human being and you will truly see only Love. Your entire truth, your complete reality will ever and always be matching up the Love "within" them to this glorious Love We are, you and I. The more you recognize your truth as Love, the more you will see it in everyone else. You will ignite for them this same route – where the Love within you has grown and grown until it merged with the Love "without" (outside of you as Me in the transcendent sense), and the two become one.

Yet you will still be able to "function here" on Earth, as Jesus did. Just as you would do now when traveling in a foreign country, you learn to speak the language well. You already know the language of the daily world, "the illusion."* You understand the "play" or the "theatre" of the illusion. You will use this knowledge as a "diplomat" from a far country. An emissary of Love. Thus will you now grow in Christ consciousness. You will now grow in this experience of yourselves as only Love. Every step will be a wonder! This I promise you.

Should you "dip" into the fantasy of the illusion, of believing there is other than Love, just remember how easily I can lift you up. Come closer to Me through prayers of Love and gratitude. ***Gratitude is your statement of trust – trust that I will always bring you back to the truth that there is no negativity at the level where you want to live!*** Then, beloveds, when you again feel My touch, surrender completely to

Love. You will be back in the realm of Christ consciousness, until a time will come when there is no smaller self with which to "dip."

This will be the day when you stand by My river of living, sparkling Love. I will take you in, fully, baptizing you as the one great truth of Love. The Dove of Peace will settle forever upon you as you will know only Love. Never again will there be conflict, ever, in any form. You will only see in front of you that which is firmly in your heart. Then, dear ones, those who come in proximity to you will be healed because you will look at them and see absolutely nothing but their truth. Your Love will bring it forth. "The illusion," the world in which you walk daily, will still be made known to you, but dimly, as if you were hearing a story. You will reach right through it.

You must be steadfast in your continual surrender to Love that I may love through you. Then, as you become only Love, there will be no "surrender." There will just be Love. Every moment. Flowing in great abundance through you, blessing and transforming everything it touches.

This is not a special path or an unusual one. You walk it only a little ahead of the others. So those who have not "caught up with you" are yours to help along. I say to you now that this is My Will for everyone. Every person, no matter what his or her history. Thus, you must always wait on the clear knowledge of My Will before you ever take creation into your own hands.

I lead you now into the next stage – praying gratitude for the complete healing of My children as if it were already in place. It is time to use this step in creation of **seeing that which you pray for as already manifest in each and every precious one.** Then, hand in hand with this comes the complete recognition of the truth of Love within them, always lending your support to this and not to the personality. Practicing this in prayer is excellent – even speaking aloud to the truth of them. Their "higher self" is the term often used for this but you must make sure to see it right within them, not way up somewhere out of reach. Rather you can simply pour our divine and glorious Love right through their illusion to acknowledge the truth of their heart.

I have given you many gifts in this Message. Please study it, for there are many layers here that you have to want to discover and to bring into your experience, into your full consciousness and of course, into your life. I am always with you. The magnificence of Love has no end in Me.

*The "illusion" refers to life in the world around us that is based in duality or dual thinking (good/evil, peace/war, Love and anti-Love). The "illusion" is that there is anything other than or outside of the knowledge that Love is the one and only true Reality.

**See the Message so entitled in *Say "Yes" to Love, God's Guidance to Light Workers.*

NOTE TO THE READER

The two Messages that follow – Praying Gratitude and The Next Step: Co-Creation Through Praying Gratitude — were previously published in *Say "Yes" to Love, God's Guidance to LightWorkers*. They are repeated here because an understanding of their content is absolutely essential to the sequence of God's teaching on Christ consciousness.

Even if you have read these two Messages before, we ask that you re-read them at this time in the context of this book. Because the vibration between the words is more important than the words, we often find that multiple readings of a Message from God augments understanding exponentially.

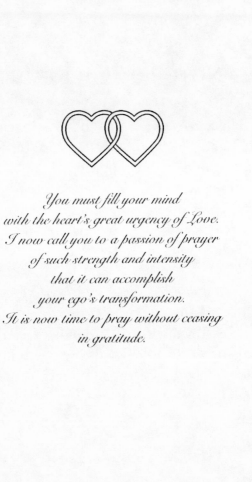

You must fill your mind
with the heart's great urgency of Love.
I now call you to a passion of prayer
of such strength and intensity
that it can accomplish
your ego's transformation.
It is now time to pray without ceasing
in gratitude.

Praying Gratitude

Dear ones, I pour My Love upon you. It is a joy to see your prayers intensify, your hearts beginning to bear the true light. It is a wonder to behold your pure longing — longing to love deeply, to open your hearts that I may love through you.

Thank you, My beloveds, for your prayers. Thank you for realizing what I am saying, for growing your hearts to encompass it. Thank you, each one, for the increase in your determination and the dedication of your Love.

Some of you have prayed to know how to become the hollow reed, how to have only the experience of My Love living in you, loving as you. You have prayed how to have only My Love in seeing every person within your range of vision. I have heard your prayers. But, dear ones, I hear the prayers of your heart long before they reach your mind, so I am ever leading you to discover the prayers that you need to pray.

What I want this message to say to you is that I know what you need. I know what you need long before you need it. Thus I even know what prayers your heart and mind must speak, what recognitions you must gain until your purpose is fulfilled.

Knowing this, ***I ask that you place your Will***

into Mine, again and again. Every hour of every day.
For though you could teach yourself everything you need
to know, it would take you so much longer. And though
you can learn to direct the various elements, the flows
and tides of life, you cannot at this level know the
majesty of My Will for you. My good for you. Even the
prayers that are timely each step of the way.

So your first step, every morning of every day and
every moment that follows, is to make sure that the
pinnacle of your relationship together with your
SoulMate is Me, is My Will. Beloved ones, without
placing your Will into Mine and releasing it, you will not
know what it even means to embody the glorious
energies that you are. I can promise that as you fully
begin to live in My Will as Divine Masculine and Divine
Feminine, you will take on the full mantle of Christ.
You will be My Love made manifest.

As you fully embody the truth of these energies,
dear ones, you will finally recognize yourselves. This may
seem to be an odd statement, but it is true. I told you
that many marriages fail because one or both people
"remember." They remember the SoulMate and feel that
the human partner doesn't measure up.

As you begin to both take on/embody this divine
nature of your charge, something amazing will happen in
your relationship and in your inner world. Dear ones,
you will recognize your partner and you will recognize
yourself. As the Divine Masculine and Divine Feminine
become expressed in you, at last the memory and the
reality fit together.

All of your life you have waited for the touch of true and tender Love and the ensuing ecstasy. Now, at last, it is beginning to happen to many of you. With it comes a deep joy. A deep satisfaction. A feeling that at last all is right with your world. How does it feel? As though you are Home in each other's arms. ***This, dear ones, is how it is going to be for every single human being as each accepts the Love he or she is, and draws forth the SoulMate.***

Many wonderful things will come from this, of course. One of the greatest, dear ones, will be a world filled with contentment. What happens when you have contented, joy-filled, loved human beings? There is no need for war. There is no drive to negate your brother, to put down your sister, for there can be no jealousy. There will be no envy. Dear ones, the entire profile of humanity will dramatically change as people experience even a little of their SoulMate relationship. Is this not a revelation? A great blessing? Is this not the doorway opening into the New World? The answer is a resounding YES. It is.

Another glorious thing that will happen as you embody the Divine Masculine and Divine Feminine is that you will recognize yourself. Now if you don't think this is important, let Me tell you that it is. Beloved ones (pay attention - it's exciting!), almost no one on Earth who is human truly loves self. I can assure you this is the truth. Oh yes, people work toward it continually. Counselors and psychiatrists, shamans and healers, priests and everyone in between are continually flooded by a stream of people who cannot find themselves in their own heart.

These beloved ones try many things. They do psychodrama. They say affirmations. They continually look at their poor parents, all of their lovers, their colleagues – you name it – trying to find a way to love themselves. Yet underneath, it does not change. Can you guess, dear ones? Of course. ***They cannot love themselves because they know what they really are meant to be.***

Dear ones, every atom of your being remembers, even if your mind does not. So here are My sweet children. They look at themselves and they see this overriding ego. They see jealousy and anger. They see scheming and comparisons. They see vengeance, be it big or little. They see anxiety, depression, desperation. All of it. And they do not recognize this being. Who is this person who is such a "mess"? Their heart cries out to them. So even if it isn't conscious, the remembrance is there, and nothing measures up. I know, dear ones. I placed the memory in you in the very cells of light that are your being. I had to. While it brings you suffering and conflict, dearest beloveds, you had to remember who you are.

So here is the great, good news. The moment you say, "Yes," to Love and your heart begins to open, you begin to recognize yourself. There is a soft sigh of relief. "Oh, thank God," your heart breathes. "I am not only that cut-off, manipulative person." "Oh, thank you, God," you cry, looking heavenward.

Now that this has happened for those of you awakening, you now come to the next step. This is where you are today. You feel your world coming right. You find glimpses of your real self. You begin to have moments of ecstasy and moments of true self-acceptance because you now see the real you peeking through. But now, suddenly, having the comparison, you really begin to see the ego. It is fully "in your face." Thus you begin your fervent prayers. And thus I lead you, for, dear ones, I too am ready. I am ready to pour through you to the world. To nurture and nourish. I am ready for every couple to take hold of Christ. To become the true light of Love. To live free of the ego.

So once again you question Me, "God, how do we get there from here?" This time, dear ones, there is an answer for you. Rather than a leap, there is a pathway. And as you walk this pathway together with your SoulMates, you will see yourselves ever more clearly. You will then find a miracle within you — a glorious circle of self-Love, a gift of full acceptance with completely open heart, first of each other, then of yourself. As your SoulMate Love blossoms, as your SoulMate touches you, your very atoms will awaken in Love. Your heart will sing exuberance as it sees the other half of itself. So Love will pour forth from you through the open floodgates. Your SoulMate will be recognized. And you will be giving. Giving of Love in your highest, fullest capacity, which, of course, brings that very Love back to you. You are washed in Love. Your very being is bathed in the warming joy of your beloved's touch. Love becomes your experience. Hourly. Daily. As you fall in Love with your SoulMate ever more fully, so dear

31

ones will you begin to truly love yourself. You will take a stand against the ego, and then powered by the SoulMate Love, you will rise above the ego, transforming it in the blessings of your Love.

This is one thing that happens as you claim your identity and embody the Divine Masculine and Divine Feminine. But there is one more piece, dear ones, of great importance. *You must transform your mind into the mind of Christ, for thought creates reality.* So even though you love in purity and even though you love in honor of your beloved SoulMate, there is another facet. There is something that you must choose to change, to gain "enlightenment." Yes, you have all heard this word used thus before, but dear ones, in this case it is very appropriate, for *your thoughts and your Love are the two ingredients of change, riding upon the energy of your Will.*

Beloveds, the ego came to life to strengthen you as individuals. It came into being to forge a separate identity. It was designed, as you know, to keep you from melting back into Me. Thus, it has surprising strength. This strength was a necessity, of course. In most cases it is not going to simply go away, even in the face of Love. As you know it has become strengthened beyond our expectancy.

When you pray to Me to be only a channel for My Love, I now whisper to you that this will be a little journey. I have spoken to you of judgment, which is the ego's main tool. And of course, the ego operates on the vibrational level below the heart.

I have asked you to pray without ceasing. This, dear ones, is the journey. *It is the choice to fill the mind in such a way that it engages the heart, and this engagement will lift you over judgment and into the mind of Christ,* which is a mind bathed in living Love. It is a mind that becomes ever joined with the heart so that judgment and ego cannot exist in it any more. It is a mind in which the heart will not allow the vibration to fall below its frequency of Love.

In order to accomplish this, I ask you to accomplish a melding of such devotion and focus that it is by your desire, your focus, your Will and dedication that *mind and heart become fused in My Will forever more.*

Thus you must fill your mind with the heart's great urgency of Love. This is the passion that lives within you. I now call you to a passion of prayer of such strength and intensity that it can accomplish your ego's transformation. To do this, *it is now time to pray without ceasing in gratitude.* Now I will explain what I mean.

Your prayers, dear ones, are beautiful. As you have swept the world, both personal and impersonal, you have prayed the most beautiful prayers. I have been greatly moved, and the angels have been sent into gales of rejoicing song. This is the truth. With every utterance of sincere prayer, with every silent prayer, which is even greater potency, oh, dear ones, everything around you is changed. You do not yet see what an impact this has had, since I introduced it as your call to becoming the Christ in Me.

So, please, bow your heads in gratitude, for that is coming next. Beloved ones, here is the truth of prayers of gratitude and in it the greatest keys for change. ***Gratitude must never be limited to what already is.***

Most people when praying gratitude (this is how we will refer to it – "praying gratitude," for as with Love, gratitude is a universal force.)… Most who think of gratitude (which of course is far too few), begin to give thanks for what they have, what is in them and in their lives. Now certainly, this is a good thing, for gratitude truly does unite the mind and the heart within you, and of course, this is a source for change.

However, dear ones, if you will remember, I have explained to you that the greatest law is Giving. Giving, giving, giving. If there is one word that creates heaven, this is the word. GIVING. Yet prayers of gratitude are usually about the self.

Here is the sweet and tender shift, dear ones. I now bring it forth to you like a princess in great array of glittering beauty. It is like the force of Love that will be Queen as you take it within you and make it the ruler of your inner kingdom. ***Here is the pathway to the living mind of Christ. It is to pray without ceasing in gratitude for others.***

Oh, dear ones, catch hold of this. Catch hold and ride it upward to the stars of your being. Let it launch you into the incarnation of your Love. And may you realize that such gratitude – gratitude in every area of your life – is a communion of the SoulMates, for the gratitude itself, which I called the Queen of our inner kingdom, is the embodiment of the Divine Feminine. And dear ones, the power of Will that sends it forth and thus brings it to life, is the Divine Masculine. So just as in physical procreation, it is the seed of the man that brings movement/life into the circle, the ovum, of the female.

So, as you pray gratitude together, in the many ways that I will show you, you are creating the Holy Family. Together as a couple you are giving birth to Christ.

Praying gratitude will become the sum of your beings, dear ones. It supercedes everything you have used to bring you here — affirmations, breath-work, all other forms of thought control, which of course were imperative to your growth. All of this was needed to bring you to the point that the Christ mind may now take root in you – or perhaps more accurately, that together you are now "pregnant with the light of Christ."

Praying gratitude for yourselves and your SoulMate is beautiful and important. But I now want to focus on praying for others, because what you give comes back to you. So as you pray gratitude for others, you are covering your own. Not that you want to skip any prayers of gratitude, ever.

Dear ones, there are two elements of praying gratitude for others. They both fall under the overarching element of "pray without ceasing." The first is gratitude for the person, or people. This is the movement into the experience of My mind. If you think about this, you will realize that this is how I think, and as you become it, you become the mind of Christ. You know that Christ is the embodiment, the manifestation in the world of My Love.

So when you begin to pray gratitude for someone, simply think to yourself, "How would God see this one, or these two, or this group?" Open to your heart and allow the experience to become you. I will lift you. I will show you this person in My eyes. I will show you how much I love them. I will show you how tenderly I love them and how any tiny opening, any little peek of hope or spiritual awareness, is so precious that I rush forth in response to support and magnify it. You will find tears of joy pouring forth from your eyes at the goodness of such recognition, and at the deep gladness I have at their presence in the world and every little opening to the light.

The more you do this, the more you will see people as they are in Love. And so you finally cease creating negativity through all the judgments you have always had as a way of relating to people. Of course, you know that whatever you hold in your mind, especially if your heart is in any way engaged, you create. Thus, most people continually create negativity about their fellow man every single time they even look at another person. Is it any wonder the world is so confused? The ego is still so strong? And, dear ones, is it any wonder people have such a struggle in growing into Love when you are all constantly bombarding each other with negative thoughts?

Dear ones, you are creating the negativity in your brother or sister's life as you pass judgment, even subtly! And because whatever is sent forth does come back to the sender (this I absolutely promise you is true), then you are creating such a difficult road for yourself at the same time. Thoughts may wound, inhibit, influence and interfere. Dear ones, negativity is rampant on Earth. As the vibrations are lifted higher, thoughts travel more easily, more swiftly. Is it any wonder then, as the population becomes denser and superficiality becomes the norm (negativity without the amelioration of spiritual sustenance), that more and more people are taking tranquilizers and anti-depressants? They are trying to compensate for the thought bombardment.

The second element of praying gratitude for others is very important. It is gratitude for their gifts. This means two things. It means the obvious – praying gratitude for all the good that others receive. This should be obvious to you – what better way to come up over the ego than to be in continual gratitude for every tiny thing that is good in their lives. The ego thrives on jealousy. People are usually filled with the ego's secret wish – for the failure of others, for their lack of success because it makes the ego feel superior. Some of you may have seemingly moved past this. To this I say that it is often only pushed into the subconscious. Whatever your experience, I who know all can assure you that the majority of humanity is still very much in this. So to pray fervently in gratitude for the good of others truly pulls the rug right out from under the ego!

The next part of gratitude for others gifts is to be completely grateful for what they will become – for what they will have as the good you know I want for them comes into their lives. This will be familiar to you. It is a form of co-creation. This is how you "have faith in things not seen." This is how you manifest good. Now you certainly should use this for yourselves as well. Thank Me for that which you have prayed to receive, thus anchoring its arrival here on Earth. You may still pray the request for the gift that you want for yourselves and others, but it should be only a small percentage of your prayers. Better, of course, is to request the manifestation of My Will for you. Once again, you cannot even begin to picture the magnitude of the good I want for you. Prayers of request have too much room for ego.

Thus to pray gratitude is definitely to put yourself in right relationship with life. It is looking at the highest vision, and lifting yourselves into the pure, proven energy of gratefulness.

As you pray these prayers of gratitude, I will be with you. For such is the vibration of gratitude that it is the most refined of current human relationship. The more you pray gratitude, the closer we will be, the more you will be filled with Me, filled with My Love, seeing with My mind, and becoming My deep loving and passionate tenderness as I lift you, My children. As you glimpse again and again just how much I love every one of you, you will be forever changed, for as you see it again and again, you will begin to accept My Love. Then you will be attuned with My heart – and Christ will come to dwell in you.

I will teach each of you, tenderly and carefully. I will place the seed within you, for the birthing of the Christ.

The only way to claim
any of the things I show you –
the qualities,
the Love
and most of all the
***Giving** –*
is to bring it into the world
in you
as action in your life.

The Next Step: Co-Creation Through Praying Gratitude

I am here, of course. I am here as joy begins to show itself to you as everything in your world. Truly, as your hearts are Love, and as you experience the deep inner joy of living in harmony with the river of spirit as it pours through you, so will your world reflect it. As you are experiencing (and you are just beginning!), when your inner world is filled with the experience of gratitude, your outer world becomes more and more and more filled with all that makes you grateful. It becomes filled, dear ones, with good and more good, for which your hearts will sing their praise to Me. Such praise of course will lift your world, refining the very vibration of your being and then everywhere you look, you will see more good. This, dear ones, is en-light-en-ment. Everything within becomes light. Everything without comes to reflect that light, which in turn brings more inner light. So it grows.

As your Love increases, as you choose gratitude, you attune yourselves to that glorious flow of giving that is the hallmark of true spirituality. So you will find yourselves sharing this experience of true spiritual family — sharing the experience, dear ones, of true and actual grace. And what is grace? It is when you accept My gifts for you, and thus accepted, the light within you and the light without are balanced, and you become the full expression of God as you.

Yet, beloved ones, in saying this, you must understand the depth of this experience to which you are called. What does this mean to live in grace? And most importantly *what does it mean when I ask you to do My Will?*

I am beginning to open this to you. I will take your hands and touch your hearts, and I will build with you a vision of who you are becoming. I will talk to you about co-creation, about what it means to be My children. Most importantly, I will open the secret chambers in both your heart and your mind and teach you what it means to meld the two. Not only what it means to gain the mind of Christ by lifting thought into union with Love. I will show you the last step — becoming true co-creators with Me. Truly, you are My children. As it is with human children of mortal parents, it is the great hope in the heart of a parent that the child will live the parents' greatest possibilities. Dear ones, My beloved heart, I now whisper to you that this is true with Me also.

In you there can be All That I Am multiplied. Can you sense this? Can you feel how this knowledge lives ever in Me – that every one of you can wave your hand across the skies and leave trails of stars and moons and planets? That you too can bring forth progeny that can hold the perfection of universes in their consciousness? Just think for one moment. If every single human being said, "Yes!" to all they are, think of how much Love could be brought into existence every moment! Oh, you cannot yet imagine it for you cannot even touch the possibilities within yourselves. But let

Me assure you, it would be great. How I cherish this thought, for I *can* see. I can see Love bursting forth exponentially, second by second – multiplying, pouring forth in great cascades. Every single mind it touches is awakened, just like Sleeping Beauty. You may smile, yet you can see the course of a potential future I am waiting upon you to bring forth.

Step-by-step, dear ones, we are building your new inner life. I am giving you the avenues for aligning yourselves to the truth of who you are – the Love that is My heart. I have spoken to you of taking hold of your heritage. Of gently, but with determination, choosing to become the embodiment of Love, the manifested heart and mind of Christ. And, oh, as you have taken this in, as your hearts have said "yes," we have moved closer. Closer. Closer. Until you can become the hollow reed and I can pour through you perfectly.

Now I bring you one more step. Where we stopped in our last exploration of claiming the Christ mind, of living as Christ, the living manifestation of My Love, was praying gratitude. Now we will explore gratitude, doing My Will, and your role as co-creators. You may ask the question: if you are turning your Will over to Me and asking to do My Will for you, as you, then what of all of My earlier statements that you are to be co-creators? Did I not create you in order to share creation? In order to have an equal consciousness who can reflect back to Me who I am in an expanded way?

I will answer this question on the highest level you can currently absorb. But please listen when I tell you that you must keep asking this question because you are a work in progress, a flower just beginning to blossom. There is no way to really show you yet all of what you can be. As you claim whatever you can understand and take it into your life to live it, only then will it begin to grow before you. Only then will the next step be revealed.

Dear ones, please remember this. Everything you learn as I lead you ever closer to Me must be brought forward into your life in order for you to know it. Let Me repeat Myself to you. *Everything, beloved ones, everything that is the treasure of your being, the truth of your miraculous heritage in Me, each and every one must be embodied in you in order for you to claim it.*

This you may already understand, but you do not yet grasp the personal nature of it. You know that all great energies must be embodied. My Love, the Christ, exemplified so beautifully by Jesus, now must be embodied in humanity, as must the energies of planets, energies of the elements and of Nature. Now you must draw this more carefully into your consciousness. *The only way to claim any of the things I show you – the qualities, the Love, and most of all the GIVING – is to bring it into the world in you as action in your life.* In other words, beloved ones, you cannot raise something up until you have grounded it as you on this (ever less) physical plane. Even great energies cannot serve if they are not embodied.

Dear ones, part of your understanding of the

miracle of the coming of Christ AS humanity is going to be your ability to see and know, to honor and work in respect and harmony with all the beautiful beings who are embodying energies for the world. For the Earth. For humanity. This is going to be part of coming awake; realizing just how deeply you share this Creation with glorious sentient beings who are the embodiment of the very energies you need to understand. Thus, instead of valiantly lifting the burden and being independent, which is the current limiting ego-consciousness, you will come into deeply honoring all with whom you share life.

It is so important for humanity to make this shift out of the egocentric human consciousness (which sees itself as the only possible intelligent beings) to the unity consciousness of the truth. The truth, beloved ones, is again far too limited by words, but your heart will experience it. It is the fact that *you are living in an extraordinary weaving of consciousness, supporting and enlightening and growing each other.*

What does it mean to live in My Will? For what I have asked of you is that you release your Will into Mine. Then I have asked you to pray without ceasing and more specifically to pray gratitude. My answer to you is this.

My Will for you is for you to be co-creators with Me. My Will for you is that you will recognize the truth of who you are. You are the embodiment of My Love already. You are My heart. *Dear ones, you already are the embodiment of My Love.* I am saying this to you so you will understand it, thus I repeat it. Please sit for a moment and take this in. ***There is nothing you have to create from scratch.*** There really is nothing you must struggle to build. In truth you do not have to work your way up through all sorts of life lessons to gain even an inkling of what you are. That is only a belief.

My beloved children, you are already it. You are Christ. You are My Love. Everything else has been a moment of forgetting, but of course forgetting with a purpose. A moment of forgetting to develop your strong individual identity so you can remain aware of yourselves as individuals without melting back into Me in bliss. The other reason, dear ones, is so you will appreciate, oh, truly appreciate everything as you awaken. If you do, if you pour Love into every single being your gentle awareness touches, you will create the New World right there.

What I want to explain to you is that I truly am giving you the keys to Christ consciousness. Coming Home, beloved ones, is truly as simple as remembering who you are. In remembering to bless every being you find before your consciousness, you simply function as a cell of My heart. This function is to allow My Love to pour through you. This, dear ones, is actually accomplished ***by praying gratitude in the form of gratitude for every being's perfection.***

Can you see, dear ones, that as you are My Love, conscious and manifested, then you have the ability to bring into the world, to manifest My Love through this embodiment? Right? This is the function of My heart—to love. So as you accept or claim the truth of your being, My Love pours through directly and you guide it through your consciousness – your prayers of gratitude.

Yet you are individuals also, the joy of My Creation. So as well as simply allowing Me to use you, which would be doing My Will, you are also to co-create. Many believe that being co-creators is to decide what you want and then ask Me to help you. It is more than this. Often those who see this way unknowingly are creating with the ego. Until every one of you, beloved ones, has completely overcome the ego, it will find truly a million ways to sabotage your very best intentions. You will start by believing you are creating in Love and before you know it you are creating separation, or creating for self instead of for others. Oh, most insidious. You may believe you are motivated by giving when in truth underneath you are motivated by getting.

If you are in any way motivated incorrectly, dear ones, it will damage both of us, for you will step forth and embody energies that are the reverse of Love, energies that are getting rather than giving. That will rob you of your spiritual life. Think about this. If you are seeking to get as you pour forth these messages, getting will come back – as empty energy. As people seeking to get from you. Dear ones, the reverse of giving, which is Love, which is Christ, is then what we would name the anti-Christ.

This is why I am so fervently growing you. This is why I now speak to you of higher Will. This is why I ask you, dear ones, to be absolutely diligent in taking on the mantle of Christ, becoming the truth of your being. *Please study, think, and practice all that I have given in these Messages.* Read them every day. Understand them enough to extract the precepts and place them in your heart.

I have told you how pure your intentions must be, how carefully chosen your inner landscape, how beautifully trained your mind, that your every thought is held in Love, vibrating the perfection of everything you look upon, thus awakening it. What you learn, dear ones, in the glorious ecstasy of your SoulMate unions will become who you are. You will embody the ecstasy that you access together. *Ultimately, dear ones, you will unfreeze this world of frozen Love just by gazing upon someone,* for your consciousness (your mind) and your held Will will be joined, and everything you look upon, you will see its truth

So to be a co-creator obviously does not mean using your smaller Will. Yet you cannot be immobilized, for truly, dear ones, it is only by living these truths that they become who you are. How then do you accomplish this? *By using gratitude to lift you into the vision of My Will for the person or circumstance you pray about and then bringing it into the world.* This can be done either by embodying the energies yourself or calling forth those who will.

Now I will begin to paint this picture in your consciousness, for you must have the whole picture. Then you will take all of the pieces into you and allow them to grow in you, especially as you grow them with your SoulMate. They will be born into manifestation in your life swiftly. Then, beloved ones, you will all be the purest, most potent magnet for Christ manifesting in you and drawn into being around you. Perfectly, and then even more perfectly. Beloved ones, the hollow reed still knows its perfection as that reed. So will you know your perfection as Christ, for Christedness is the nature of your being. Knowing who you are, you will shape My Love as it pours through you. You will mold it in the shape of Christ. Thus will you blend your Will and Mine.

Now what on Earth does this mean? What does it mean now in your precious lives? What does it mean in your moments as you seek to clarify our inner landscape? It means that *praying gratitude with passion and energy will lift you up over any influence of the ego.* As you pray gratitude in deep sincerity you are aligning yourselves with every law of Love. *I am speaking here of the praying of gratitude that is passionately grateful for the perfection of each person and for every bit of good, every tiny bit, that they receive.* This gratitude, dear ones, is first of all GIVING, for you are giving your Love and giving your blessings. You are giving your generous wishes for their highest good, and in doing so you are seeing that good. This then is the perfect enactment of the process of co-creation.

In this very process there is a fail-safe device. As you pray gratitude, dear ones, and do so genuinely, I will always come to lift you higher. I will always come, because essentially in doing such a process, you are "linking up." You are connecting yourselves right to the real electrical circuits of My heart. You may picture this as a cell of My heart coming alive. Beginning to flash! To light up. And first, of course, I am going to notice! Secondly, as you (this cell) get more and more charged, the sparks flying from you will eventually make contact with the nerve impulses or electricity of All I Am. In other words, you will then be "plugged in." Plugged in to Me and to all the energy that is life. Believe Me, dear ones, this changes everything. *So, dear ones, in the process of praying gratitude passionately without ceasing you are absolutely assured of doing My Will, not your little Will.*

As you pray gratitude, really pray it, you are lifted up, you are connected, expanded, and in this state you will see My highest Will for whomever or whatever you are praying gratitude. It will simply be there in your consciousness. You will grasp in an instant the full picture of their highest good. It will be BIG. Bigger than you could have thought. It will be connected, for you are now connected to All That I Am. You will see all the ways these connections will work to lift and heal and benefit.

Then, dear ones, having received the vision of their truth, you will help to manifest it. You will come out of this passionate prayer of gratitude with the mold of their highest truth. This, dear ones, you will gently continue to hold forth for them. You will bring it into the world. Using the sacred Womb of Creation, you, together as SoulMates, will bring it to birth. Thus, dear ones, will we co-create.

Now this will also work for creating for yourselves whatever you want for your life, dear ones. The difference is that by using this pattern you will be assured that your Will and My Will are one. You will start by praying gratitude as if the goal were already accomplished. Fervently. Passionately. *You must not stop until you can feel yourselves being lifted up over the ego into the alignment with My Love.* Then, in this union, you will see what My highest Will is for you in this area. · Then you will set about manifesting it, bringing it into embodiment in the world. I can't stress enough how important this is. The coming of Christ is the Christ consciousness coming to dwell in you, My beloved ones.

So you see, it is you who can and do choose the topic or the area to pray about. This is co-creating. But the difference is the next step. *You place it in the pattern of manifestation by thanking Me for its perfection while waiting on the revelation of My Will for this area, person, situation, desire.* It is this, dear ones, that is the key. You will receive this vision, this experience of knowing the highest truth. This I promise you as long as you genuinely pray gratitude with your heart. Then you will see the perfection of Christ – the manifestation in perfect Love for that being/situation. In Love you will help bring that higher truth into the world, accomplished by your merging with Me through giving with your heart and thus receiving from Me the real truth of Love to be manifested.

I will continue to open this path wide for you as we travel the way of Love and the awakening of the mind and heart of Christ in and as SoulMates.

NOTE TO READER

It is requested that the next two Messages, *Abundance and Co-Creation: The Principles and the Steps* and its companion, *Abundance: Living the Will of God* be read in exact sequence (not out of order).

Your crowning glory
is in the power of your being
to co-create Love
and to push it forth.
It is the great sign
of your truth as My heart
that you alone
are the generators of this force.
With it you may also nourish life.

Abundance and Co-Creation.
The Principles and The Steps

Love is a living thing, and abundance is its natural expression. Love, dear ones, is who you are. While it is an experience of glorious ecstasy as it flows within, as it opens you and frees you, it is the fact that it is generated by you that is our focus now.

Here you are, My precious children, waking from your long slumber. You are teetering between the worlds, one moment swept up in ecstasy, the next believing the world you see before you. It is into this delicate balance that I come to begin to build carefully an ever-clearer vision of where you are meant to live. I ask for your heart as I do this, for the only way this can truly guide you is for Me to become alive within you.

Yes, beloved ones, you are dancing between the worlds. So one moment I must tell you that everything is dependent on your ability to choose the New World. All your life and all your energy must be dedicated only to reaching the other side, to making the leap, to claiming the prize of a new consciousness.

Yet in another moment, beloved ones, you stand before Me, your hearts open wide, afire with truth, your glory blazing forth from you — rending the veil instantly. In such moments you are ready to begin your new life and the tools must be there, in your consciousness the moment you arrive, for you to lay hold of, to claim as your own. So we will build for you a functioning map of your life as you claim it and live it in Love — as you make it into the new consciousness and begin to learn your way around.

Please remember, dear ones, that these messages are alive – alive to the needs of the moment, alive to the process of growing into a different kind of consciousness. So please do not believe that any one is the complete or final answer to a question. Every single millisecond you are grown, and in the moment that follows this one, you may be ready for a bigger piece.

So, this said, I now begin a dialogue with you of living Love on the topic of abundance, for this question lives so close to everyone as you seek to move from the illusion of lack into the world of truth. I will bring ever closer to you the great truths, the fullness of My Love and of the glory of your real life. Then each of you must come to Me to experience this living communion and to bring these truths into your deepest self, knowing that even as you stand forth in the most glory you have ever touched, there is always more.

Faith is also a living thing. It is time, beloved ones, to take your faith in Me and the fact of the abundance I so desire to give you, and prove it to yourselves, in form, in front of you. It is true that if you place your life in Me, I will provide for you. But you are now reclaiming your true selves, and, beloved ones, you are creators. So I now ask you to move beyond the infant's trust in the parent, beyond the belief that I will provide, into the actual experience of creation.

You can see how this will bless you, for it will anchor the truth of who you are in your lives in such a way that nothing will be able to shake it. If you know without a doubt that anything you need or want, you yourself can bring forth, would this not be the revolution of Love of which we dream? For suddenly only you would have claim upon your world. You would be free to place every thought in every moment upon Me, and upon the New World we are creating.

Faith is believing. Mastership is demonstrating. We are moving into Mastership — into the actual upliftment of this world, of this life, of this heart and this body, into a world of ecstasy, a world of the living movement of Love.

It is time to live your destiny. Since your destiny is as co-creators, then every success of creation affirms your truth as nothing else will.

Abundance is a natural result of the movement of Love. Love is passionate. Love is filled with the "heat" of life. It is like the noonday sun upon the plants. All things grow as it touches them. And you, dear ones, are touched by Love

Love is generated. We have spoken of this in the context of SoulMates, and for all of you your SoulMate is the answer to the greatest facility for the generation of Love. You can always connect with your SoulMate, always, whether they are with you physically or not. Yet

Love can also be generated by each one of you in every moment, by your Will, for Love is the substance of your very being.

Once you truly feel this generation of Love, you are ready to begin the process of co-creation. I say co-creation, for we are creating together. It is My Will for you that you be creators, and it is My Will for you that the abundance of Love is yours always, through all of life, on every level, forever.

Beloved ones, I tell you that this process is as natural as "falling in Love." It is a part of who you are. I also tell you that it is as immediate as you are present in the vibration of Love. This is why I ask you to place the development of your faith in the New World, the crossing from the old mind to the New, first. But this is only one step.

Oh, My precious children, I ask you to demonstrate the New — Love as an active principle. "Faith" too is a living, joy-filled reach for our communion, for the place in you where you can move it forth into action.

Thus, I do now ask all of you, while holding yourselves dynamically in the absolute trust of your full presence in the New World energy, to begin this practice of precipitation, of manifesting. Once you realize how simple this is, you will be free. Free, dear ones, to manifest your Love tangibly. Free to express who you are perfectly in the world. As the world is lifted beyond the veil, there will be no further impediments to Love.

There will be no clouds of negativity to slow (to a crawl) the clothing of our creation in form. Instead, you will begin to live your freedom as do those in higher dimensions.

So, beloved ones, I ask you to take a moment. Take a moment to picture your world now so that you will know you can express who you are in form. Now, think of nothing else but your highest expression of your nature. As you create together with your SoulMate, I can promise you a synergy of Love and Will so perfect that each of you will have absolutely everything that expresses you.

I say this so you will understand that in your truth, in real Love, there are no compromises because there is no need. In the higher nature, your expression is also a living, dancing, moving thing filled with luminous joy. It is difficult for you to imagine, but please do your best. As you both pour forth your vibration to manifest every beauty of who you are, the two are blended in a living art of Love. You are surrounded by an environment that perfectly expresses both of you — blended, yes, but fully you. Nothing — not one atom of your expression — is sacrificed, yet something new is created from the two of you.

So practicing now, please trust this process of Love's expression. Trust, too, for this moment of exploration that there are no boundaries, no barriers and nothing is solid. This is very important for your joyful success. Beloved ones, you are only working with energy, even here in its densest form. Keep working with this expression of you in your heart and mind. Be sure it is projected equally by the two. You can even see it before you, if you wish, equal distance between you — the position of the SoulMate womb.

THE STEPS TO CREATING

The foundation to co-creation is ever and always the giving of Love. The more Love you have moving through you and outward as you serve your beloved humanity and Earth, the easier and more instantaneously you will create. Thus, beloved ones, may you always fill your days and nights in the greater service of loving the world. This Love pouring forth from you is Love that comes from Me.

1. *To this stream of Love coming from Me, please add your own.* Pour forth the new Love that you generate. Do this with your SoulMate, even if you do not see them manifested in front of you. As I have said, their presence in your life is fact. While each of you certainly can generate, it is amplified exponentially in union with your SoulMate. It is also your statement of faith in their presence (actively shown, as faith must be) and will bring them forth more easily.

2. *Create the form.* Create this clearly, holding the image as you will it "below" the flowing river of Love that pours through and from

you. Use whatever attitude assists you to make this image as clear as possible. You can picture the "building with clay" analogy, for this may help you see the form of what you want to manifest as your Love expressed around you. You may simply visualize. You can use words, sounds, even outside props like photos, but get as clear a picture as you can.

3. *Hold it up to Me. Do not fill it with Love yet. Do not clothe it yet with living substance. Beloved ones, because you are still in your dance between the worlds, you must be sure this is your highest truth.* You do not want to manifest an impediment. In the radiating energy of that stream of Love, it should be easy to get a reading of its accuracy, to feel My presence close to you or answering within. This part is very important.

Your lives, those of you reaching for Christ Consciousness, are given to the holy purpose of awakening the world, and this step, beloved ones, is the difference between the little Will and the higher Will. The difference between that which truly expresses the New and that which keeps you in the Old World. You may ask, "Wouldn't it be safer to withhold this process? to allow God to simply manifest my good?" My answer is a resounding, "NO," because of who you are. You, beloved ones, are My expansion, and once you are beyond this veil of time and ego, you will know these things. You will know always who and what you are and you will create new worlds in ecstasy. You will add to My Love, add to My Creation. But as you now begin to cross this divide between the worlds, you must listen carefully to be sure you are in alignment with your truth. You may also come to this process having already received your vision from Me. Even then, go ahead and hold it up to the brilliant light of flowing Love, for in doing so it is energized.

4. *Fill the form with Love's energy and clothe it with the substance of Love.* Dear ones, now it is easy – for you have created a river of Love flowing through you. You have created a stream of your own generated Love to add to the existing Love. You have been feeling this stream with your desire to love, to serve, to feel divine Love. Now lift up your form into this glorious stream of living, moving Love.

Now you bring the form to life! Oh, this is a great moment! For you, beloved ones in this moment lay claim to your true nature as My children. You accept your true power. You acknowledge that this power is ever and only Love. You affirm, in this action, that Love is both the life and the substance of absolutely everything. And so, acknowledging this, you hold up the form of your creation into the stream of living Love that is moving through your being, your life and world. Whether you are creating an object or a healed and sacred world, the process is the same. See it energized with Love – not as substance but as ecstasy – as the shining moving living light that pours forth from the movement of the substance of Love. Oh, see it illuminate your creation! See what was an image become a vibrant, living thing, filled with the light within which is the movement of Love that animates all things. Oh, dear ones, feel the energy take hold! Feel the spark of life be lit within it. Then see it lighted in animation, as are you – a living expression of Our Will and Love.

5. **Then, dear ones, clothe it with the substance of Love.** You have filled your creation with the movement of Love. Now coat the outside with Love as substance. Do this by removing some of the Love from the river of Love flowing through, and allow it to cool enough, to stop moving enough, to become a tangible substance. See it forming a shell of sorts around the bright animation of Love's energy within it. However, do keep it flexible! You don't want to lock it in to a rigid encasement. You do want to bring it forth in the world, but you want to keep it in the New World level, where it is fluid enough to be very open to life and to the glorious interactions of the loving cosmos. Dear ones, it is My hope that having

thus created, you will rise up to meet our creations at the level of the New World vibration – rather than the necessity of bringing it all the way into this level of density which we name the Old World. However, it is important enough that you become free from the tyranny of lack that if your creation does not manifest after sufficient time, you may return to this moment and slow it down further.

6. ***Concentrate and consecrate.*** These steps are the same as ever given, for they are imperative. As you grow into the assurance of your divinity beloved ones, you will easily manifest instantly. But until you do (which means until you are living fully in the New World and completely and totally in your heart or higher self every moment), you will need tenacity. You will want to love your creation, to feed it and reinforce it, to cherish it and, most importantly, to consecrate it to Me and your expression of the truth of your being. Thus,

7. Every day, just as you would tend an animal (do NOT forget to feed it!) that you cherish with your entire being, just as you would tend a garden of the most rare and precious seeds, ***set aside a regular time to come back to your creation to amplify the Love. To tend it, nurture it, and visualize it coming forth.***

Dear ones, once you begin to have success, this will become shorter in duration, less and less days, until you literally will reach up your hand, holding forth your vision, animate, clothe and bring it forth instantly, for you will be living in My highest Will for you. There will be no need to check and you will have such Love flowing through that one thought will fill and one thought will clothe and one thought will bring it forward into your manifested life. You will also be living at ever-higher vibrations so it will have less and less distance to travel down the scale of density to meet you where you live.

8. **Seal It.** Dear ones, every time you come to visit the moment of your creation, you must close the door when you leave. This makes sense, doesn't it? You do not want to leave this sacred chamber of co-creation open to any and every other energy that want to come in! You must care for this sacred space very carefully, and especially for your creation that is gestating. Thus you may use whatever imagery you prefer, but seal your creation while it makes its way into birth in the world. Wrap it in light or picture a special chamber with a door you close. See it in a bejeweled container, as big as needed. Remember even a whole world is small in the grand scheme of things! And be sure to close the lid. Whatever is right for you. However, just as a seed must sprout

through the soil, be sure your creation can push free when it is ready to manifest.

And, beloved ones, two other things. Do not give anyone else the door key. You know this, of course, but it is very easy if you are deeply involved in this to tell someone about it. Now I will clarify that if you have a Soul Family or group who creates together, you certainly can share with them – for you know they will amplify with you and never ever throw doubt upon the fires of your passionate creation. And of course, absolutely you must share your creation process with your SoulMate. Use your SoulMate womb to amplify if you did not start the creation together. If you are not yet recognizing your SoulMate with you, speak to him or her anyway. Speak to them in the etheric, for I can tell you this. You will be attended by your SoulMate even if it is only their higher self while their body is sleeping. But this attendance will occur and means everything.

Beloved ones, in all of this you are continually leaping into a new concept of reality. If you falter, go back and re-decide your truth. Raise up your energy. Then come right back and attend your creation. Do not allow yourself to believe that any backsliding into the Old World can possibly affect you negatively. Remember, you have the door closed in your creation chamber. I can tell you, the belief in the "damage" is far worse than the little bit of negativity released, which you can easily transform with light – violet or otherwise.

Last, dear ones, but definitely not least, please do manifest your abundance in your life as well as manifesting a healed and holy Earth and a larger elevation of Love. Here is why I say this to you again. The two largest tyrannies perpetrated on human consciousness are (1) that sexuality is always a negative energy. (Now remember, it can be an energy of anti-Love if manifested below the heart in ways that cut people off from Me.) It is the "all inclusive" consciousness that is the subtlety often engaged to corrupt My beloved humanity.* And (2) that everything is outside yourself, especially your supply. Supply of money definitely. Oh, dear ones, this belief is such a tool of anti-Love. But it also has been applied to your supply of anything – supply of Love (you have to wait to "find" it), supply of joy (comes from something you'll be able to "do" eventually, etc.)

We are reclaiming all of it. Reclaiming it is claiming it as your truth. The truth of your being. The truth of My Love. The truth of our relationship. The closer you come to accepting this truth, the easier this process will be. As with everything else, it is shifting your belief, shifting by choice where you believe your life comes from. **Soon you will all know absolutely unequivocally that your life comes from Me, as does your Love and your abundance.** Then, oh, beautiful ones, you will prove this to yourselves – and the moment you do, you are free.

I want you to experience these truths, beloved ones. So, yes, it is important to first put away everything except the shift of your belief. But then, dear ones, you must actively engage. Love is a living creation, filled with crackling energy, waiting for you, beloved children, to direct it forth from the God in you. The truth of our union. The perfection of Love. There is nothing faster to get you here than your ability to see, to feel, and to touch the results of your living, active faith in Love. Let's begin. Listen. I will whisper your highest truth every moment.

*See **Say "Yes" to Love, God Unveils SoulMate Love and Sacred Sexuality.**

It is time to choose the New World —
to "act as if," as you say.
It is time to live and move and
have your being in the glorious expansiveness.
It is time, dear ones,
to place your precious vision
totally on perfection.
It is time to know the truth of Oneness
and understanding this in fullness,
you will be My heart manifest in the world.

Abundance.
Living the Will of God

Many of you are beginning to hear the symphony of life. As you look out on a rainy landscape and you can feel the exhilaration, the joy of Nature as it bathes in the waters of life, it is you breaking through! It is you breaking through the veil into an experience of the Real World.

We are calling this the New World, but of course, it is not really new. Instead, it is the world that has always existed in its perfection in Me. But without humanity it is not complete, and at last, to My greatest joy, it is time for its completion. It IS a New World for humanity, as distinguished from the Old that still lives all around you.

Now I further deepen your understanding of abundance. Oh, dear ones, how humanity longs for this freedom. How humankind groans under the oppression of the terrible perpetuation of the lie of lack. But as I teach you precipitation, as I teach you manifestation, as I teach you how to come back into Love with Me, there are many things you have still to learn. It is in this learning that the keys will be given, the keys to the freedom of My beautiful children.

So I come very close. I hold you most tenderly. I say to you that this is the beginning of a great work that will free My beloved ones from the tyranny of separation from Love and free them from the insidious lie of lack. This material on abundance will have no compromises. It will be written in flaming letters of truth that even most of you do not yet understand. Neither will the rest of humanity really understand at first, but *I can promise you that the very fact of the existence of these messages of truth about SoulMates and abundance mark the end of the reign of the anti-Christ, the end of the lie.*

Trust, too, that these are living messages and that even if they sit upon many bookshelves interminably, there will come a moment when these messages will speak. They will call to the person whose life they honor and they will hand him or her the key to the cell door, the key to the prison of the illusion. These messages contain every layer, so that as a person grows, every reading will be a living unfoldment of My Love and Spirit.

I continue to expand your understanding of the awakening of abundance in your life. Oh, beloved ones, let Me draw you close to Me again. Please open your heart. Can you feel the truth of this? If I Am Love and you are My children, then I could never, ever create a life of lack! Would I not provide every abundance, all good and wonderful things?

Think of how you love your own children, dear ones. Even if you do not have children you know the truth of this. Every human parent wants every good thing for their children, if they have Love in their hearts. In fact, the greatest sadness, the most constant prayer that rises up to Me is parents' wishing, longing, praying, to be able to give more to their children.

Well, if I Am God, and I Am, then I certainly am not limited. If you are My children and I your parent (we will use this analogy for a moment), then certainly I can provide all good for you. Obviously. Then what has happened? *The answer, of course, is that you have forgotten who you are.* You have forgotten that you are children of God. You have forgotten that I have waiting for you absolutely every good and perfect thing — abundance beyond imagining, a life of joy. A Love for you that is personal in its tenderness. I ask you now to remember this. I ask you to remind yourself continually of who you are. Every thing depends on it. Not, dear ones, on an intellectual belief. *Everything depends on your personal emotional experience of our relationship.*

Until you can accept this, accept how I love you, accept who you are – until it becomes the reality of your daily feelings – you cannot have the abundance that is waiting. Not really. I have given you the precious keys to manifesting, to claiming your place as co-creators with Me. Yet today I place another vision before you so you know where you are going. Then I will build the daily pathway to get you there.

I have just given you the vision that you, My beloveds, can claim your heritage and can manifest your own destiny of light, life and loving abundance. *Yet here is the caution. What is born of the Old World will live and die in the Old World pattern. What is born of the New World will have life everlasting.*

If you lay claim to your power of precipitation but you are still in limited consciousness, then just as any physical plane birth, so will your creation be. It will come forth with effort. It will live, grow and delight you. But there will be ups and downs in your relationship with it. And ultimately it will disintegrate.

If you lay claim to your power of co-creation while living in the New World, your creation will manifest as instantly as does a feeling of deep true Love. It will always grow from blessing to greater blessing as it gives of itself, forever. There will be no end to its good, and the Love of which it is made will always draw to itself more Love. This, dear ones, is the difference between the Old World and the New. It is the difference between the ego and the heart. It is the difference between your Will and Mine.

Here is the law that will give you safe passage to the reclamation of My gifts to you. You do have to "lay down your life in order to claim your life." Not, dear ones, the physical life, but the personal life. In other words, at this point in your growth, your evolution, you really truly cannot see the extent of your good, the extent of My gifts to you. You cannot, beloved ones, even begin to grasp your heritage. Who you are. What you can be. *So at this moment, in order to claim your gifts, you must give your Will over to Mine.*

Doesn't this make sense? If you can't even begin to grasp the good I have for you, or who you really are, or how much you can love (oh, you have NO idea!), then the only way you can get where you want to go is to let Me take you. Yet, while this seems so obvious and so easy, it is actually very difficult from where you are in the Old World consciousness. Some of you are learning. You are claiming this truth, but still there is wavering. And still there is no capacity through your human consciousness to even begin to grasp what I have for you.

So I have given you the steps of manifestation. Now do I ask you not to use them? No, but I do want to remind you again and again (oh, you may get very tired of these reminders) that *every conception will manifest exactly the seed of which it was conceived.* Thus, when you come to the step where it says, "Hold your creation up to assess whether it is in accord with My Will," this step is ALL-important. This step is everything. This step, dear ones, could take you years. In other words, do not pass over this lightly. Rather, you must develop deep discernment. You must listen in every way for My affirmation. You must travel the path diligently until you are sure before you proceed. So when I give you these steps, please know that this is where your co-creation is most important – for co-creation means in My Will. Do not move forth until you know, beloved ones. Do not move forth until you know.

In the past, a few mistakes – well, "no big thing," as you say. Isn't this world completely full of such mistakes? (Oh, the answer to that one is yes.) However, this has changed. For you are standing forth,

My blessed children, ready to make the leap. Ready to shift from Old World to New. So you cannot afford mistakes. For you to now bring into birth a misconceived creation could be the difference between staying stuck in the Old or moving forth into the New. It could be the difference between continuing the illusion or the dawning day of clarity as the clouds part and the light of your own truth blazes forth.

Thus, let Me speak to you about your creations. For even you, My most "advanced" LightWorkers, are still mixing your worlds continually. You long to have financial abundance and you long to do naught but serve Me. Where is the dividing line? What is the right use of your creative powers? Are some things "good" and others not? How do you discern?

Here is My answer. *It is only when you completely trust that I want every possible good for you, and thus you completely and totally give Me your life, that you will be in right relationship. It is only when you are so totally joined to Me, in Me, of Me, encircled by My Love, living in the continual light of My close and glorious upliftment, that you can truly use your gifts. It is when you are so joyously aligned with Me that every breath is worship and every moment total Love — only then, dear ones, will you easily reach up and fill the cup of your creations with the living waters of Our flowing Love and bring forth every good for others. Then, beloveds, you will be blessed. You will be blessed with every gift, every possible joy, all riches, all good, all vibrant joy-filled health. All of it.*

Now your heads are spinning. Why would I even bother to give you this process of precipitation, of manifestation, if it might be "misused"? Because it is time. Because you are having more and more and more moments when you are lifted into My Will, more moments when your co-creative powers are truly right for you to use. And (listen carefully) it is time for you to instate this process so you can direct your energies when you are not quite in the spirit, not quite fully uplifted. Beloved ones, if you are lifted up and you receive My Will clearly, you know the power of our communion. You can use this process to keep focusing your energy when (if) you are not fully in this communion. So do you see? *It is the beginning of a process that is a hallmark of your new life — the creation of good in My Will.*

Now let Me speak a little more about this step, the all-important aspect of giving your Will to Me. Your little mind, or old mind, or ego, will say to you, "Well, if we are co-creators then we should create. What is this 'Will of God'? And what does it even mean anyway?" It will push for you to evaluate what is your highest good. But, oh, how far, far short it is. If you listen to it, you will be robbing your own self of your inheritance, and I must tell you, it is better than an earthly inheritance of wealth. You may have to wait a little while to claim it, but when you do you will be amazed.

Being in My Will is different from having faith. Having faith is essentially seeing the world as it is and believing that I will work it all out for you. This is essentially the Old World version of being in My Will.

Being in My Will is completely letting go of every definition of the world, the life you want, who you think you are, what you believe I want from you. *It is waiting on Me in everything.* It is becoming the hollow reed, the blank slate; but it is becoming this in My Presence, in My light, in My guarantee of safety and Love. It is leaping into My arms – not into the void. Be sure every moment that you give yourself you can sense My presence, feel the light and feel My Love surrounding you.

I ask all of you to pray deeply to understand this. To understand My Will to give your life, to give yourself, to Me; to give service, to give Love. Give. Give. Give. Give. And only then will you be ready to receive.

At this point in your spiritual lives, beloved ones, you must give without ceasing. Then and only then will you be ready to create. You notice that I have said in the previous message on precipitation that first you must have in place the flowing river of moving Love. This will only and ever come from giving. Giving forth of all you are and most importantly giving yourself to Me. Give your life to Me. Only then will you have your life. But then, dear ones, then you will have your tools. You will know that in giving you receive.

So what will happen? Your creations will be blessings for others. And *beloved ones, when this becomes your greatest desire, when truly all you want is others' good, then you will know you are at last ready.* You are in My Will. Then, dear ones, with glorified presence, grace and true humility, I will lift your hands into the stream of Love. I will fill your life, fill the mold of your perfection, and create for you every amazing and abundant good thing. Nothing of the Old World will be in you anymore. And you will see, dear ones, that truly your Will has become Mine. You will step forth in the New World upheld by glorified Nature, supported unerringly by the manifestation of your Love, and fed completely on the fruits of your labors – the giving that has become the center of your world.

Trust Me. Do not trust appearances. Even those that seem obvious. None of you know another's agreement with Me, and to ever believe that you could possibly evaluate anyone's progress, including your own, is your immediate and obvious signal that you are operating in your ego.

Are you ready to give yourself to Me? This is the moment of Christ in the desert. I have given you the tools to precipitate what you choose. In these two messages on precipitation, I have given all you need to lay claim to the riches of the world. Having given them, I now place before you the decision of how you will use them. *Will you use them to precipitate your version of your highest good? Or will you wait on Me? Will you give Me your life so completely that I will use you as the perfect creation?*

You see, Jesus did not always look like the Christ. But he was. Every single moment. For he allowed Me to do his greater work through him. I guarantee it did not look like the Christ of God upon that cross. At any

moment, Jesus had the power to work his own Will.
He could have said, "Well, surely this does not look like
an example of the power of God's light!" He could have
blasted forth and floated free, above that cross. But he
did not. Why? Because he gave his Will to Me. And
in doing so, he saved a world and proved later that the
Christ stood forth in victory over death. As was
My Will.

It occurs only as you finally love enough to allow
Me to love through you, however I want to. You
cannot know in your little mind what My greater Will
is to be. You cannot know whether I plan to use you as
I did Jesus, to be a visible example of the power of
uniting your Will with Me.

Yes, it is the moment for these messages on
abundance to go forth. Why? Because there will be
signs and visions from everywhere, many of which will
be the temptation. There will be messages saying,
"Create money; create your great life; use your newly
awakening power for …" It will be a dangerous journey
these next few years. It must be clear what is possible
and what is being offered. Yes, My children will have
many choices before them.

Oh, dear ones, to those of you who do know this
great Love and who rest in it, this is My call to you.
Every true light must go forth to do My Will quickly.
But first you must understand the temptation. You
must understand what is before you. You must
understand that even for you, My clearest of
messengers, the temptations are great – and very, very,

very well disguised.

Beloved ones, be careful. You can (and very often do) have two thoughts at once. Some of you are learning to see this. You can have a thought of truth and hiding beneath it can be another thought – of the lie – canceling out the truth. Oh, it is subtle. Yet I must show you – it is imperative. I must show you how it is I love, how perfectly I lift you up, how only I can clear the field and bring you forth as My daughter or son. Only thus will you create the world which we both hold dear. Your freedom, beloved ones, is what I bring. Just will to do My Will. Then will all My Love be yours.

Dear ones,
this is where I am taking you —
back through the Garden gate at last,
back into the Eternal Now —
before judgment,
before dichotomy,
before "good and evil"
ever crossed your mind.
It is only when your mind is one,
only when you see only light
that you will be Home.

Abundance.
The Pattern

Dear ones, please know that there is absolutely no conflict in what I have given you in the two previous messages on abundance. If you believe that there is, then right there is the line for you of the Old World and the New, the old mind and the new life that is lived open to the flowing expression of My Love, My heart, which you are.

I have elaborated the steps in the precipitation process and I have shown you where you must be to precipitate clearly, to precipitate the world of Love, to manifest My Will for you. I have stopped your little mind from rushing forth to create its vision and thus to take you further from Me, rather than closer, closer to our real Love, our true and glorious relationship.

Beloved ones, notice the trickery of the ego. How easily it skips the steps, grabs onto what it wants to see and hear; what it wants you to believe in order to continue its existence. The very first step in the precipitation process is to create a river of giving — of flowing, living, singing, serving Love going outward through you. Outward. Stream – river.

Selfless is the key word here, as is the word giving. Dear ones, you could spend a lifetime here.

Right here. Creating this foundation. Building your Love until all you can do is give it. Building our communion until every particle of your being lives only to give. Only thus will you have the right vibrational energy to create. Do you have this? Sometimes. Only sometimes, and then it is often fleeting. It is not your every living breath. It is not the continual prayer rising up from your heart to Me. Even if you wake in the morning asking Me to use you for the blessing of the world, by lunch you have forgotten, and all that is in your mind is the babbling brook of your little self, not the great and glorious flowing river of outgoing Love that is your true nature.

Every thought of self is still the little mind, even when those thoughts are spiritual. Of course, your ego is clever. It knows you are dedicated to light. So it places before you the vision of *your* healing, *your* light, even *your* ascension. Yet it is the lie, beloved ones. I can promise you that no one has accomplished this by focusing on himself or herself.

The law, beloved ones, is this. *As you give, so will you receive.* Remember this. Know that when you have, with greatest tenderness, brought other children home to Me without ever thinking of yourself, then you will be ready. The ascension is our reunion. It is the moment when our Wills become fused. It is the moment when you are the Christ, the Love of God, made manifest. You know this, dear ones, if you know nothing else — that I Am Love given forth unceasingly, given forth for all eternity. Thus only as you become this also will you come to understand your own reunion with Me.

Do you see how subtle the shadows are? Dear ones, there could be legions of LightWorkers focused on themselves and they would not know Me. So in giving you this greater awareness, I am leading you very carefully. And dear ones, there is a rhythm in this, too. I give you the vision, and then I teach you how to bring it into your life. Have I not always done this, for as long as you have been listening? This is no different. I give you the vision. I announce the coming freedom — freedom from the lie and all the veins of its oppression. Then I show you what it takes to claim this as your own.

There is a truth of Love now growing in you, a union of your Will in Mine. In these moments, your entire being is filled with dancing light, and you know. You know you are in My Will, for you can literally experience My Love pouring through you. You can feel it rushing outward, giving to all the Love that fills their need. It is a Love that seeks out every heart and makes its way in through any crack. It is a Love that is gloriously attended by the natural world — Love that makes a difference in ways your little mind could never imagine.

In the ego self you cannot participate in this glorious river. *It is only when you stand with completely open heart that the river of My Love can use you.* Dear ones, when you are lifted, when you are joined with Me, you know. You know the coming shape of the New World. You know how Love will manifest.

And you know your "piece," as you say. You are sure of it, with a surety that nothing can shake – a surety born of holy communion with Me. ***This is the time to precipitate.*** To add your Will to mine. This is how we co-create. In doing this, beloved ones, your vibration, the signature of your being, is woven into My perfection, My Will for the glorious rebirth of Love. Thus will there be new Love created by the fact of your participation.

Ultimately, when you have grown into your fullness, you will add your own creations to this. Dear ones, you will create all of the details of the New World! Oh, but you will have the iridescent colors of true light to work with. And you will have the song of God always living in you, and everything you do will be for the blessing of others, for the joy of creating their surroundings, those who share this world with you.

There is a different mind being born in all of you. Call it higher mind or mind of Christ, but whatever we call it, you will recognize it. ***It is opened by giving.*** It is awakened through release into the higher Will. It is nourished, fed, watered, and brought forth, as you are bathed in the river of My moving Love as you reach upward to participate. As you join in the flow by the conscious choice of unity, of Love, and most of all, of giving.

Then, beloved ones, it will become your greatest desire to give. Then you will precipitate correctly. Then, My awakening heart, your life will become the flowing river of increase, for as you give so you receive.

How do you precipitate your daily bread? By giving others theirs. By establishing within yourself that glittering, glistening water of life; by making way for My giving through you, by putting aside the little self who ever sees getting – not giving – as the way to having. By reaching forth your precious hands, by holding in your higher mind, the image of a world well fed. This tender desire for nurturing My children, pouring forth from out of you, will then create a vacuum that, by law, will draw energy into you at the level of what's given!

Do you think that giving forth these steps of precipitation will be met with this understanding? Of course it will not – because even many of you still vacillate. So please remember – all of you who are reading this on whatever page, be it handwritten message or book – that you must set the pattern here. That as in all things, it must be brought forth into the world by those who are incarnated here. Thus your work is given. This is My Will for you made manifest as you read between the lines of this message. In you must My Will be done that for every person coming after you there is the understanding that it has been done. Dear ones, it is you who must do it.

Therefore, *I do give to you the keys to the kingdom. Then I give to you the deeper truth of them.* Surely, if you think about it with your heart, I would not give you a means to create more of the same. That would make no sense. No, I give you the process to bring forth the New World. But you must first understand the spiritual truth. Where we are going is a spiritual world, a world of Love, of blessings unlimited.

I have been given your assurance, you who serve Me, that all My children will be with you as you rise. Ponder this. I have taken you at your word, and your word is given, blessed ones, even if your little mind has no memory of it. So there must be a way for it to work, right? There must be a way to get all My children from here to there. Yet look around and you can see the level of illusion in which so very many live. It is through these messages that I am growing you into your role.

Dear ones, it is in these messages that you will see that there are spiritual laws that will make this work possible. Yet the only way you can access them is to give yourself to Me, to allow the higher Will to release you from your ego and from your false perception. *You must allow the mind of Christ to become your mind – knowing, dear ones, that the only path to Christ consciousness is service. Giving.* Yes, being the hollow reed, but more than this. What you have yet to understand is the active partnership of living My Will.

You, beloved ones, are living here. In the world. In form. It is through you that I reach for My children. So here is our partnership. You allow Me to establish in you the river of Love, as I pour My Love through you out into the world. You give your whole and holy self to Me, completely. Only thus can you be free of the trickery of both little mind/ego and the forces of the anti-Christ. In Me you are lifted up, in exhilaration. In the glory of giving Love. Here you "stand upon the Mount" of our union. All heaven is yours, all the world is yours to bless. Here, without personal Will, living only to give, you will hear Me. You will know My Will for you.

Knowing My Will you will place every resource in its service, including the law of precipitation. Thus will you form the vision on this plane of what I have given you, and formed, you will fill it. In greatest joy, in ecstatic union, together in Me and with your SoulMate (be they visible to you or not), you will give your heart completely to the fulfillment of this work. *Give your heart. Give your Love. Give your service. Love My children, above all else.* In this, beloved ones, there can be no mistakes. No creation of impediments to your own service/awakening (such impediments would be a tragedy, dear ones, for you are so passionately needed).

I ask you now to notice further. Once you know My Will for you, once you see clearly the avenue of service, you are a part of it. You are fully and actively involved. You are giving your piece and manifesting this giving passionately, for this is how we co-create. This is how I reach through you, how I use you to bless and awaken My children. Now I call to your attention the greatest and most important difference. *Doing My Will is an active participation.* It is adding who you are to the picture, the vision. It is using your presence here to bring into manifestation My Will in you, as you in the world.

For many people, doing My Will is a passive experience. They believe they become that "hollow reed" and that's it. Nothing to do but sit back and wait and keep affirming My Will and just see what happens. Nothing could be further from the truth. You are a unique creation. A piece of My heart. Thus, how My Will is done in you and as you, is a unique, beautiful expression. Like the snowflake, every one of you is an exact and individual pattern. You are meant to be the co-creators of an expanded reality of Love. Together, as SoulMates are rejoined, you form the heart of the New World. So I send forth the blood of life, of Love, and as does a heart in every form, you are to give it forth.

Reach up. ***Reach into the stream of Love I am pouring through you. It is there. Amplify and add to it.*** Then, becoming that Love, you will know how that Love is to pour forth through you. You will know, in a communion of Love that lifts you far beyond your little mind — out of separation into a unity of giving that is the truth of life. From this place you will create.

Some of you already know. You know your piece; you know how truth is to speak to the world as you. Yet you have not yet actualized it. It feels so close to you. Why has it not come forth? It will not come forth until it can be brought to birth in the New World — brought forth to an eternal life rather than being birthed into an Old World form which will live a while and die.

So dear ones, I am showing you. I am shifting your consciousness. Purposefully. Carefully. I am giving you the vision, but just as you reach forth with an Old World mind to take it, I bid you stop. Come closer. Let Me show you how to bring it forth into life eternal.

Into the world of Love rather than the world of self. This, dear ones, would be "pearls before swine." It would be trampled on by the ego selves before it even lived very long.

Many of you are very close. But you must be willing to be contained until I pour you forth. If you pour too soon, the pouring will be wasted. If you are anything less than in My higher Will, you could pour your wisdom into the hands of anti-Love. Trust Me. Trust Me to grow you, step by careful step. *Go back. Re-read these messages, for in these I am growing you into the vessels of higher Love to be held forth by My Will rather than your own.*

It includes prayer without ceasing; gratitude, praise and Love; a living dialogue with Me until you are dissolved in your little selves and lifted into Love with Me. The hollow reed is only one part. Then you become the hand of God, reaching forth into the world.

You must have the tools so at every moment you are ready. Then when we are joined as one, I can show your heart just how I want to love the world, and you can bring it forth.

Do you see how careful we must be? How easy it would be for you, living in this world of illusion, to mistake your little mind for truth? To have ego convince you that you were saving the world only to find you had been failing Me instead? You have seen this, beloved ones, in those who are "fighting darkness" and who energize it instead. At this point you cannot be too careful. Yet you are so close, dear ones. You are able to rise into My greater Will. You can let this flood of Love use you to reach My precious world. Then dear ones, take hold of the tools and use them to bring our vision forth. Since you are not yet a permanent resident of this higher world, the New World of Love, I ask you to check yourself, to proceed with care, to develop greatest discernment – that you not be one who builds up the darkness while believing you give light.

You will know. You can begin with those things you are sure have come from Me. I certainly have been telling you over and over for years. You do know what to trust. Your heart has verified your truth, the truth of who you are. Your aim will be true. Your work will commence. It is in giving that you receive and as you give forth that which you know is My Will for you. It will open you very quickly to more and more and more clarity. Just keep checking. Keep attuning. Keep lifting your vision. You will feel My blessing. You will have verification. Just don't proceed until you have it.

Proceed when you are in the flow, when your vision of the New World is so close it is lapping at your feet. Proceed when you can feel the tender hearts of My children receiving you. Proceed when you can touch them in your spirit and you know that I Am in you. Proceed when the longing to open My children's sweet eyes is your motivating force. Then, dear ones, you are ready. Take no thought of yourself. Only Love. Only give and the law of giving will take care of you. For hundredfold, "yea, more," will your giving be multiplied. You truly do not need to give it your attention. Yet you can use your needs to enlighten you, for I can tell you, if you have lack, it is in an area where you need to give.

Remember this, and every moment will bring new consciousness and the awakening of the truth of Love, and that is who you are.

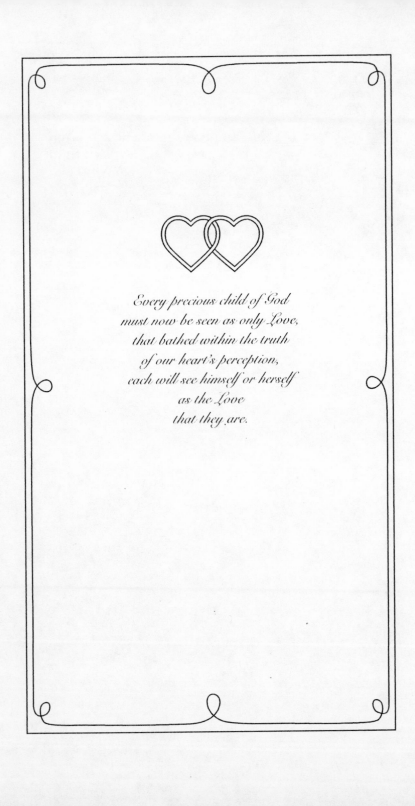

Every precious child of God
must now be seen as only Love,
that bathed within the truth
of our heart's perception,
each will see himself or herself
as the Love
that they are.

Abundance.
The Bridge of Gratitude

Let Me speak to each of you, tenderly, intimately, at the very deepest level of your heart and understanding. I ask you to trust that to every heart, every sweet mind, every hand that I prompt to turn these pages I speak personally. I know every heart that is now opening like a precious flower in the increasing sunshine of My Love.

It is the depth of the grace, the light, the spiritual food for My beloved children that is so needed. This I must bring forth. Dear ones, you can read platitudes everywhere, even real inspiration. But here I give you everything. I grow all of you daily, hourly, moment by moment, specifically that I might speak candidly, passionately, and at a level not ever yet brought forth. Because how can we bring forth a New World, how can we awaken in every heart the New Man or New Woman, unless everything is made new. This is what we are doing.

So when I speak to you about abundance, I am not giving what is already known. I am carefully, so carefully, building the foundation, bringing forth the experience of the New Heaven – on Earth.

Let Me give you all, My precious children, My assurance that in these two areas - Love and abundance or prosperity - lay your greatest chains, keeping you bound to sadness and lack. Let Me tell you also that you have been purposefully and carefully programmed to be bound in these two areas. Why? Because these are the areas of your power.

Love, dear ones, is the essence of your very being. It is the nature of who you are and the passion inherent in all of your true abilities. Where is it in your life? Buried. Buried under piles of ego and generations of lies and pain. *I bring you back, beloved ones, to the remembrance of your SoulMate and the truth of Love. I bring you back to truth not only as your nature, but of the ever-present manifestation of that Love in your life.*

And abundance – oh, dear ones, the travesty of this! How could you ever believe that I would want for you a world of slavery to lack, of days spent, for so many, "eking out a living," and an entire planet full of people underfed. Not only food, but self-respect – oh, that is by far the greatest loss!

So here, upon these pages, I put forth the keys to freedom. I will also tell you that at any level they can be used, these pages, these keys, will bring you freedom. So use them, as you will. To give you reassurance, I do want you to know, all of you who read this, that you can find within this book the keys to every freedom, including what you name ascension. *Yet at whatever level you understand, and however clearly or unclearly you can perceive My Will, I now encourage you to move ahead.* Take hold of what you can understand, what you can believe. Place your hand in Mine and dedicate your heart to Me, and then proceed. Proceed to manifest your daily bread, literally, if that is what you need. Trust that any and every step like this that brings you freedom from the lie will bring you closer to Me.

Some of you may have wondered why I gave the steps and then proceeded to caution you about using them. That is because there are deeper understandings here. For those that want them, they are offered. Yet they will still be here waiting when the basic needs are met, and they will be easier to access once a person realizes they have some GOD power. I refer not to the false power of the ego so exalted in the world. Not the "power" of some people to make money while others right beside them are starving. No, *dear ones, GOD power, which is glory and abundance filling both heart and plate until both are running over.*

Thus I say to each of you that I have brought you here. Here to this moment, these words, this understanding. Now let Me show you in another way how your cup can "runneth over" as your heart is filled with joy. In this I give you the bridge. The bridge between the life of illusion and the perfect knowledge of My Will, where moment to perfect moment, you fill the cups of your molds of desire with the substance of Our given Love, and manifest instantly the ever higher and more perfect world.

I have given you the steps and then I stopped to deepen your understanding. Now I start the flow again with the praise and joy within your hearts. Here, beloved ones, is the answer to growing close enough to Me that *every thought is held before the light and brought into alignment with My Will before you ever choose to bring it forth.*

The bridge to your continual manifestation of the gloriously perfect life and world is singing praise and gratitude. Beloved ones, two things happen when you pray gratitude. You increase all you are grateful for, and it brings you ever closer to Me. Dear ones, in order to sing praises to Me, in order to pray gratitude continually, you must be looking at Me. So this of course means that I become the focus of your attention. I have always told you that you are co-creators. So *in praying gratitude and singing praise you will create more of Me. More of My presence in your life.* More closeness between us. More of the vibrations of Love, more of the movement of light and joy, beloved ones, is the natural state of your feelings when you are in My presence. And feelings — well, dear ones, they are the energy by which you create.

So, my beloveds, I call you again to praying gratitude continually. Oh, I can barely begin to paint for you the beautiful results. Now I will elaborate on gratitude in the context of co-creation; manifesting; precipitating your highest good.

First, there can be no mistakes by using gratitude and praise (of Me), for in doing this your Will is focused on Me rather than on a specific thing to manifest. Of course, your attention then will draw Me forth, will bring Me ever closer to you, where then you will easily perceive My Will. And then, once perceived, you will use the steps to bring it forth easily.

Notice My use of the word "easily." Beloved ones, this process of precipitation is natural – as natural to you as life. It is not difficult. It will not take great effort if you are in My presence. Instead it will flow forth from you with the ease of a clearly held visualization. It will be held up and filled, then brought down into form as simply as you read this sentence, when you are in My Will. And, beloved ones, the fastest way to our continual experience of My living presence in your life is to create within this singing upliftment of joyous gratitude.

Thus, this living, breathing gratitude becomes your inner landscape. Oh, please, dear ones, understand this simple process. This is where you are to start. It is easy to create, create, create, and create it until every moment you are filled inside with this ongoing experience of praying gratitude. Yet even to say "praying" may create in you a sense of effort. Your goal must be that it be effortless. That it bubble up from your heart continually, filling your mind, your body, your being, your world. Yes, you will need to prime the pump at first. You will want to establish it. This would be the praying gratitude. Pray it until it becomes the natural process within you. Then, beloved ones, all else you do will take place in this beautiful atmosphere of living gratitude. Gratitude will become your approach to everything. It will become your home within, dear ones – a place where you go to be upheld in My Love.

And your preparation will serve you well because this living gratitude will refresh. It will assure your being, including your mind, of your truth. It will be the doorway to ecstasy as surely as your SoulMate will.

Then, dear ones, when you have gone beyond the need to "pray" gratitude and into the ongoing experience, then you can begin to use it to go further across the bridge. However, please be sure your gratitude for what you have is established firmly first. In other words, it has moved beyond praying gratitude into living gratitude as the very essence of who you are. Then, beloved ones, we can move closer to the moments where you will bring forth in Me everything you decree.

First, one digression about gratitude for what you have. There will be people who will come to you and tell you they have nothing to be grateful for. (Begin to pray for them immediately.) To all of you who might feel this, I must say that we are speaking here of co-creation. While it is My intention to now place in your hands the keys of conscious creation, dearest ones, you are always creating! Thus, *if upon looking at your life you have nothing to be grateful for, you must stop right there and take responsibility.* This I must say to all, no matter the level of understanding. Any who feel that way – that their lives hold nothing for which to pray gratitude – the very place to start, of course, is to find gratitude where it could not be seen before! Oh, this is so important.

You must start with gratitude for what you have. Even those of you who believe you can see beyond this, for very few have this gratitude as the continual experience of life. I ask you to have such gratitude singing within you as you lay your body down at night. Have it fill your dreams, your wakeful moments in the night. And, oh, when you wake, make it a passionate response to the blessing of a new day. I did say "make" it, for this of course is ever your choice. **You**, beloved ones, paint your inner landscape.

Until you live in gratitude for what you have, there will not be the impetus we want to bring forth new things. Notice that I did not say you couldn't bring forth new things. Just that there is an energy, a movement, that we want to establish.

It is to this foundation of ever-present gratitude – of pure and glorious amazement at the miracle of life and your existence as My beloved heart (is this not enough, truly, for eternal gratitude?) – that we then add. We add the giving forth, for the energy of gratitude is the energy of the real world of your permanent being, rather than the illusion of lack and effort. The energy of gratitude is so filled with dancing light that you cannot keep it still. You cannot contain it. After bathing you in its exhilarating joy, by its own nature, it pours forth. It moves outward in gratitude for all around it. This must happen naturally, again, as your continual reality. When you have built enough gratitude within for your life, it will absolutely have to pour forth. This is the beginning of your river of giving!

Do you see what I mean about effortlessness? In

every step of the reclaiming of your real life, there is a flow so natural that it truly does have its own life. Once it is established in you, it lives you. It generates. It has its own life and it brings with it the next phase. Just as a seed sprouts and every phase of the growth of the plant follows perfectly, so, too, does My life within you grow also. For it, too, is a natural thing.

So once your inner gratitude comes of itself to flow out of you, to rush forth to bless and notice the ever more expanded world and universe, you will have to start giving. Giving Love, blessings, teachings, time, whatever is right. Still you have the ever-present living dancing light of gratitude as the foundation for everything else. ***It is the gratitude itself that will naturally bring about the giving.*** Dear ones, remember, gratitude is a feeling. This is very important. It is not a mental list, a "mindful" prayer. It has little to do with the mind. The mind may be useful in naming things you are grateful for at first, until the gratitude itself takes over (and it will). But without the feeling, we will definitely not get where we want to go.

Thus I remind you that this process is worth everything. I have given you the steps to precipitation – to providing for yourself and for others the world you want. You can certainly use these to bring forth more of the Old World – and even this would be fine, because it would carry with it a self-respect and freedom that would bring you back to gratitude. So however you begin, you will get here. But please stay here, becoming the living experience, the glorious feeling, of gratitude continually. Do not stop before you accomplish this.

Then, dear ones, as the gratitude overflows on its own and the river of giving begins, then you are ready for the next step of gratitude which is gratitude for what you will have as your full, perfected self. This, beloved ones, is the last step before the natural reclamation of your true ability to precipitate in My Will for you. Oh, as the glorious dancing passionate joy of gratitude pours over and gives of itself to all the world, begin a new prayer of gratitude, based in your heart, for the perfection of Love that you are now becoming. Only leave the "becoming" out of your prayer and just issue forth the glorious song of praise. All you have come to understand will be yours as a Christed being, as My perfect Love living in a world of Love.

This, dear ones, begins the resonance process, the feedback from Me, as you get closer and closer to claiming your ability to fully co-create. Now remember, you are creating constantly, right now. The world around you is the result. Yet in this phase, you now are in communion with Me. I can promise you that your looking to Me in gratitude through the first phase will absolutely establish our glorious communion perfectly. So now, in this phase, you will begin to give praise for what you are becoming – although in present tense, of course. As you breathe forth your vision of your perfected self, you will receive My reply. You will receive either instant verification or the feedback of the true awareness of what you are, in truth. This process will be exhilarating, for every discovery, every communion, will fill in the missing pieces in the great vision of your spirit. These visions will include your SoulMate, for they cannot do otherwise. Thus they will, as well as aligning you, begin to manifest the plan for the two of you in your joined destiny.

Thus, beloved ones, will you build, step-by-step, the true understanding and the passionate Love for who you really are, and for what you are to fulfill as My manifested Love, as the glorious piece of My heart that is the two of you, as one. Once you are here in glory, fullness of joy, ecstasy long enough, the very same thing will happen. Of its own accord, this ever more passionate, light-filled knowledge of yourself will begin to live you. By its overflowing movement in your being, you will reach up, fill the mold of this knowledge with moving Love (giving) and bring it forth effortlessly. You will know how, for you have the keys. You know the process. Yet it will be natural, as if you have always known (and you have, of course). It will simply spring forth in joy.

When you reach this point, these things will then manifest very fast, almost instantly, for all the energy has been building through your passionate daily living of gratitude. Pieces will already have been coming forth around you. Then suddenly it will seem magical. Click, click, click, piece after piece will form until you are the living Christ.

"Take no thought of what you will wear, or what you will eat," for remember, you are My children. Would I not care for you even more than the lilies of the field or the birds of the air? Of course I would. But do you know the main difference between Nature and humanity? Nature lives in gratitude and joy. Every

Nature spirit is painting the glory of their being, expressing passionately who they are in Me. Every moment. Truly, never taking thought for any moment but the now. Resting in the assurance of who they are in Me. Should the form of this change for them, it matters not. Forever and always they are in Me and they know it.

This, dear ones, is where I am taking you — back through the Garden Gate at last, back into the Eternal Now – before judgment, before dichotomy, before "good and evil" ever crossed your mind. Do you understand the message of this? *It is only when your mind is one, only when you see only light, that you will be Home.* Then you will be back (as were Adam and Eve, the symbols of the eternal SoulMates) here on Earth in a Garden of Paradise where everything feeds you Love and light and every experience reflects only who you really are.

Dear ones, it is easy, for it is My Will for you! This is all it takes for you to return to the choice of perfection, the experience of only Love. Please, beloved ones, no longer be deceived. The dark is never part of you. Nor is it a natural part of Nature.

This I can tell you. You will never see the truth by looking without, for everything in the current world reflects the current humanity. Thus does even Nature reflect to you the erroneous perceptions of yourself. When you come back, dear ones, to the living experience of your truth, led there by Love and gratitude as explained, you will ascend effortlessly also. You will not even know you have accomplished your ascension.

All you will know is Love and ecstasy. *You will note that you live in a beautiful world where all around you only grows, only blossoms, only radiates perfect Love and beauty.* Your manna and theirs will be the fruit of the Tree of Life. Have you noticed this? Even with all the recording and translations, this statement remains true. It never was or ever will be the "tree of life and death."

Thus you do not any longer need to make your peace with darkness. As you dance to the sweet music of Nature and honor the moon and her season of feelings, know that in the Eternal Now, in the world of peace I am bringing, there will not be decay and death, and there will be the change of seasons only at your request. And then it will be instantly.

I paint for you the truth. The world of duality is passing at last. Freedom from the tyranny of lack, dear ones, is coming. As I place before you this vision, you might think, "Only in Heaven does this exist." I will then remind you that Heaven lives inside of you.

I take your precious hands in Mine and tenderly bring forth your heart. Your true heart. Your true world, that reflects only your true heart. The lion will lay with the lamb and every form of life will be in glorious conversation. Not only among themselves — as they are now — but with you. Just remember gratitude, and we are on our way across the bridge. *Gratitude is a feeling, and feeling is the energy that creates.*

So I, with so much tenderness, am guiding you in

ways you cannot even see. Thus we circle around, from gratitude to gratitude, to gratitude again. And every time, beloved ones, it will take root more firmly and live more fully with you. Remember the way of Love is easy. It is natural. It is true life. Thus will each step gently bring forth the next until you are exalted, precious beings, Home in Me forever.

When you look at
what you still perceive
as outside of yourself,
soon it will make that shift
that is the hall mark of Christ consciousness.
All that you have believed was "without"
is actually within.
The truth of Love I Am
is a web of life so strong,
so full,
so perfect in its holographic nature
that everything is Making Love
with everything else.

Abundance.
God's Garden Is Our Consciousness

Abundance. What is the difference between your goal and Mine? When the topic of abundance, manifestation, first takes root in someone's mind (someone living in the world), it is usually money that is the focus. How to solve the continual dilemma in your lives of livelihood, supply, and prosperity? Yet in these pages, dear ones, I have a different goal (as you've noticed!). It is because I am preparing you to manifest the New World.

Beloved ones, your precious minds are the tools by which we will bring Heaven back to the Earth. *Your minds are the incubation chamber of a new consciousness — a new consciousness so different that when we accomplish it, you will have no idea how you ever survived life in the old.* It is to this end that I ask you, please, to make the study of these messages on Love and on abundance the most important thing in your lives. In Love, as SoulMates, you become the generating station of the energy and substance of the New World. In the shift of your consciousness, in the precious chamber of your minds, beautiful, glorious children of God, pieces of My own heart — it is there, in your consciousness, that you mold that Love, that you bring it forth.

Yet here, in this world of shadow and confusion, how will you find and how will you hold the images necessary? The changes you are bringing are beyond your normal consciousness. It is in answer to this question that I pour out these messages on abundance. The abundance you really seek is far beyond money! It is the abundance of light, of power, energy, joy that you will become, in which I can then plant the glorious vision. This will be our co-creatorship. *In the beautifully prepared field of your consciousness, I will plant the visions of the New World as the Heaven that is meant for you. Then you, together with your SoulMates, will bring it forth.*

Beloved ones, you will bring it forth instantly, moment to moment. I will place the vision in your consciousness and I will bring it forth through you, because you have asked to do My Will. You have opened your hearts in glorious ecstasy, the energy of life. You have established the generation of Love with your beautiful SoulMates. Thus everything is in place. Can you see the vision I now plant within you? A world, here, right now, within the old world in which fertile hearts and minds are waiting all around the planet. Prepared. Open. Filled with light. Generating Love. Living in glorious joy and ecstasy. Then, in one moment, I can plant within everyone the truth of life, the awakened world, and as a unit, all together, effortlessly we bring it forth. Then, joined together by the streaming bands of Love connecting every one of you, the rest of humanity can be lifted as you allow My vision to come forth.

Can you feel the joy of this, dearest ones? Can you feel how well prepared you will be, how very carefully I am growing you in the understanding of your higher life? This is a life in which your personal needs are given easily to the higher good thus giving Me your hearts and minds to use!

This is where we are. This is what I call you to. Oh, certainly I could show you how to bring forth personal wealth but it would fail you in the long run. It would, as I have explained to you, come and go by the simple fact that the seed of its conception would be the thinking of the old. Truly, beloved ones, once you know the power of Love that is your heritage and the joyous praise that will be our life, you will be able to bring forth anything you want, instantly. And you will, as you build for the rest of My precious children the world I have always intended for you.

You will be the builders. This is what I train you to! Can you allow Me to place this vision in your mind? Can you imagine the joy you will have as you cover the Earth, bringing forth all good for every single person on this planet? As you teach and love each one, as you show them how to tend their garden – both the garden of their inner self and the garden in which will grow the light-filled food to nourish their bodies? Oh, this will bring satisfaction and joy so far beyond anything you could create yourself, or for yourself, that there is absolutely no comparing.

Beloved ones whose hearts are Mine, I have begun "planting you." I am filling the fertile soil of your precious dedicated lives with My vision.

We have spoken of gratitude, of the living, singing joy of praise, and I have told you that such an inner life will allow you to know My Will. I now lay My claim to the most powerful gifts that you can offer Me. What is this that you can give that makes every piece of our plan come forth? It is this very garden of your mind.

Dear ones, as you reach for Me with open hearts, as you fill yourselves with longing to do My Will, then it truly is into your imagination, your mind, your consciousness, that I will place My Will for you. I will give you the vision of what to bring forth. Then as I do, as naturally as you breathe, as easily as you love, you will use the steps of co-creation and you will bring it forth.

What does this mean in your life? It means holding forth your consciousness as a light-filled cup, empty of the little self, and allowing Me to fill it. It will be easier than you think. Because as you fill your consciousness with the singing praise and gratitude, your vision is on Me. Thus you will be lifted up beyond the little daily mind. *Your consciousness will become golden light while your heart takes over with the praise and gratitude.* Remember (this is SO important!) that gratitude is a feeling. Thus, though your mind may need to "prime the pump," it is your heart that will ultimately take over. It will become an uplifting, an opening, an inner flow of ecstasy that will be simply ongoing – an ongoing rejoicing within you. (Remember this word – rejoicing). So, beloved ones, lifted easily by the vibrations of gratitude, your mind, or

114

consciousness, will be open. Available. Waiting for Me.

I will come and plant the visions. Oh, dear ones, what a joy we will share. What a communion of being – for in these moments you will know that I am both without and within you. You will feel and see and know every part of what I am showing you. A total experience of the whole of it; the feelings, the knowledge. As you keep rising in your consciousness, you will also see in that moment of conception the entire scope of its total connection throughout the world.

It may start small. It may begin as more personal, as I give you the pieces of your Christedness – how that will look, how that will feel. Then I will plant the ever-widening vision. It will be a part of you, increasingly, until you are receiving Me continually. Dear ones, I present this awareness because it is so important. *The heart does not function alone. The heart and the consciousness are intimately connected in this process of co-creation.*

The chalice of your consciousness may be seen even more clearly as the golden SoulMate womb, the place between you where you bring forth the creations of your union. Yet this process is ongoing and I want to establish it in each of you – so every moment you are available. So very quickly we can move completely beyond the little mind of ego, because certainly (urgently!) we have to clear your precious consciousness.

Dear ones, you are generating. You are generating Love. You have ever more light flowing through you. So you are creating. Now. Ever more powerfully, even from moment to moment. You can feel it. You know that your light is increasing. So you can certainly see that it is urgent that we remove you from the ego's reach immediately.

One thought with any emotion behind it and it is done. Created. Especially, beloved ones, as you live ever more fully in Love. In a sense this Love elevates and protects you, yes. But if you "slip," as we say, then you are certainly creating. You may not see the results because you do have Love as your ever-fuller reality. But the thought will manifest – most likely when picked up by another spiritual person who is still really wavering and who will draw your thought form to them!

This is sobering, since your hearts are so beautiful, so dedicated oh, so precious to Me. This is why I am teaching you and growing you so intensely. So you will draw close, ever closer to Me. So the Circle of Love that is our pyramid (the SoulMate couple and Me) becomes your only reality. Ever. Until these messages become a beautiful loop of light that pours through you continually, growing you with every round. I have told you that these messages are layered carefully. Thus as you read them, you will anchor this light in your very being. You will set free the electrons of your mind and you will become a dancing living song of praise inspiring the entire galaxy.

Beloved ones, how I reach for you. We meet in your heart and in your consciousness. It is these two that are the center of the new universes that you will create. It is these two that feed and grow each other. It is the seed placed in the womb of your consciousness that becomes clothed with the substance of your living Love and, joined in Me, goes forth as Mine to live eternally.

There is a plan, dear ones, that cannot fail. Its cornerstones are you. This means, beautiful beings of glorious joy, you cannot fail. Yet you must realize how important it is now to become the fertile consciousness that is ever Mine to seed and to use to bring forth the greatest good, oh, way beyond your imagining.

It is obvious to you why I must seed you, for of course, you cannot see this glory without end, and your consciousness is ever meant to wait on Me for this. But the little mind, the ego self, has completely cluttered up the gardens of human consciousness. So that, truly, My seeds cannot even find a place.

Now your brain, dear ones, is nothing but an electrical signaling system. It is meant (or we should say its true counterpart, the higher mind, is meant) to draw into it those ever present electrons, those cups of light of which I've spoken.* When functioning perfectly, the brain helps create a field of light – truly! Our garden analogy is perfect, for this is the higher truth. Thus all throughout your consciousness is this pristine golden light, waiting for Me to use it. Waiting for the vision. Once received, this dancing light, these electrons, rush into position to carry forth the creation. Serving as the energy or light that the nature spirits use in a physical garden, this light is the life force of your creation. Now you have the vision, and the life force to enliven it. All that is needed is the actual substance with which to clothe it, to bring it forth. That, then, is your Love and is why your heart and consciousness are so close, beloved ones – so close.

Every idea is meant to come from Me. Every idea that is accepted into your consciousness is a conception. A seed planted. Whether you see it as garden or womb, it is there. If your consciousness is filled with ego thoughts, there is no room for the real purpose of your consciousness. Yet still the creative process marches on. The seeds that are planted are then enlivened by your fear or your feelings brought forth in an un-awakened consciousness. So the creation is not instant, not as powerful, but it happens – as is so obvious by your current world.

As you praise and fire your heart with gratitude, beloved ones, hold up the cup of your consciousness. See it simply full of golden light. Then trust. It does not matter how long you wait – for I am waiting, too. I'm waiting until the field is ready, rich and fertile with your Love and gratitude. Trust that your consciousness is Mine, your imagination made for Me, as the tools of our co-creation.

Then when an idea comes (at first it may not qualify as vision), entrust it to Me. Even if you aren't sure that you feel My presence in it, just give it forth and say to Me, "God, you bring this forth." And know that I will.

Know that if you keep your consciousness clear, waiting on Me to fill it, that the filling will continue. Often in the beginning, your vision, first planted dimly, will continue to come back to you, each time more clearly, until at last it is ready. Know, beloved ones, that I will bring it forth perfectly. Then let it go and wait on Me. Beloved ones, as you do this and you begin to see these ideas manifest, you will understand ever more clearly how we co-create, for you will see yourself in your creation.

Switching now to the analogy of a human birth – the conception is perfect in Me, the Holy Child of your divinity, but it is the substance of your Love (generated with your SoulMate) that builds the form. So you will see yourselves in it. You will recognize how it feels like you, this beautiful new creation. Yet it will be perfect, always, for I am in charge of it.

Beloved ones, let Me seed your consciousness. As you live in Love, as you give your Love as blessings to the world, you live in a world of increase. Thus will all of your creations bring great abundance forth for you. You truly do not need to take thought for your provision. Yet you will need these keys of co-creation so you can provide for others who cannot provide for themselves. In doing so, you will provide for yourself, effortlessly.

I do tell you that as you grow in Love you will use your Will only to give, for it is your holy nature. Only in giving, will you feel right; only giving will feed your spirit. And in losing yourself (your little self), you

119

will find yourself (your truth, your Love, your perfection). Trust that you will feel this, passionately, even if you do not feel it yet. It will come quickly as the little self is superceded. And superceded it will be – easily. There need be no struggle, where you wrestle with it and work to subdue its incessant commentary and judgment. For, beloved ones, if you establish living gratitude and praise of Me, your vision is ever upward, upon our Love, upon My grace. Very quickly this will become your only reality.

This is what we are calling Christ consciousness. It is the glorious experience of the truth of life, no matter what your outer self may see before it. It may take a little while to establish this as your absolutely exclusive reality – thus I ask you to make this your focus. Just as you prepare the soil for the glorious food and beautiful flowers you bring forth in physicality, so also must you prepare with care and diligence the garden of your consciousness.

Oh, lift your precious thoughts to Me, then let them disappear in bliss as the joyous song of ecstasy fills every part of you, for gratitude produces ecstasy as surely as does your Love because all roads lead to the same place!

Yet even before you are there, dear ones, treat every idea as a holy one and give it up to Me. Know that I can bring it forth perfectly even if it is not fully formed of light. As you trust that each idea is Mine, you will be excited about seeing what comes next. You will then feel the quality shift, for you can't miss My presence with you. Soon you will know My signature of light and everything else will fall away. I trust you, dear ones, to be dedicated. Thus you can practice and I will respond because truly if you decide to allow Me to bring forth every idea in its highest perfection, you will quickly manifest a perfect life.

Do not make this difficult, beloved ones. Do not make it difficult, because I can tell you that when you are in My light, in My presence, living your truth, for the first time ever things will be effortless. More and more so, as you grow in Me as one part of this process flows joyously into another. From grace to ever greater grace. From joy to ever fuller joy. Oh, from exuberance to passionate celebration of life. From ecstasy to ever greater ecstasy.

As you go through your days, keep returning to the dancing, living song of gratitude and praise of Me. Come back, come back, come back, come back until no matter what you are doing, this gratitude is all you feel. Then, dear ones, we are on the road to freedom!

Ecstasy at night, gratitude throughout the day. So shall your lives become. In the glorious union of your SoulMate Love, the very atoms of your being come to new life. Freed from the substance of the shadows that have filled the spaces in your very atoms, you become the freedom, the dancing light of Love. With every washing in ecstasy you become less physical. Your atoms reclaim their mobility. The electrons can come in and deliver their light.

Then rising, you lift your consciousness to Me that I may do the same – fill every thought with golden living light, prepare the living soil of your consciousness. Oh, how amazing your days will be! Dear ones, you have not ever yet felt bliss! The very best feelings you have ever had are as nothing, precious children. Oh, the joy I have for you. Oh, the presence of the living light.

When you are wakened, beloved ones, every single moment will be utter amazement. As you see another human being, you will see them as I do. You will be filled with the marvel of their creation. What a gift of life, what an incredible experience, as your consciousness as mine, touches them. You will not see through the ego's eyes again, ever. You will see right through the lie, into their precious heart as conceived by Me. And how will you do this? Through our joined consciousness. Through the fact of your Christed existence, ever and ever a living part of My expression, yet even more than this.

And Nature – oh, the miracle! Every breath will fill your entire being with a sweet nectar, a light. You will feel it bursting forth within you to nourish every single cell! You will feel the light delivered to your body. And every moment your spirit will be joined in the singing expression of joy that Nature is ever experiencing.

Nature will teach you to paint with the skies, to create life instantly, blossoms popping forth around you, sweet soft grasses springing up before your feet. In the singing gratitude of your hearts in union with your

SoulMate and the clear golden consciousness waiting for Me, I can continually plant the vision of perfection. And you will bring it forth. Thus, moment to precious eternal moment, everything in its full glory will manifest around you. There will be no need for you to plan it, to envision it, to hold it up or seal it, for that process will have become your nature. Thus, *at every single moment, I will be using you to hold in place the perfect world, for I will be able to feed it through for you to create, moment by moment.*

Little by little I now begin to paint for you the vision of your true and perfect life. The vision of your natural state. Thus I am already planting with tender care the truth that will come forth through you. You will always have it in you. Then as you say, "yes," as you accept your truth, this seed now planted will spring forth. Heaven and Earth – you won't tell them apart. At last they will be one and the same.

Beloved ones, please be willing to allow My seeds being planted in you to remain and take hold. *Truly, as I have told you, there is no way to get there from here. There is no progression from Old World to New, for they are not even vaguely similar. Thus it is only as you allow this vision of the true world to be born and you choose to live there that you make the leap. Making it, you create the way for others to leap as well.*

Thus will you see ever more clearly the perfection I can work through you, because only those of you who can allow the planting of their consciousness can possibly begin to uphold the vision, so that I may fill it.

Everything good you have ever dreamed of is so paltry in comparison, beloved ones, that all I can possibly do is ask for your consciousness to allow all possibilities. If you create any definitions, any parameters, any firm concepts of what we are calling the New World, right there you limit it.

So allow your consciousness to be an open thing. Allow Me to fire your imagination. But even then, do not define anything I am planting, any vision I have sent. Let these also be a living experience of the magnitude of living Love. Only thus can you possibly be ready to think big enough.

If you find yourselves in your little mind or egos, just push away. Lift up above the gravity. Not gravity of the physical type but gravity of consciousness, for everything in the ego is taken with great seriousness. Just leap back up into My waiting Love. Should you have any trouble blazing out of the pull of gravity, begin to imagine the greatest things, the most amazing, most powerfully good, and then begin to multiply them. This will lift you back into light where everything dances with openness. It is here, in the golden light-filled consciousness that you will begin to see life as it really is. Here you will see life as dancing particles of light interacting, flowing in and around each other in a fluidity of movement that will take your breath away.

Keep reaching, beloved ones. No more ordinary consciousness. No more daily life vs. spiritual vision. This must now be your continual decision.

We will have a partnership – a partnership of miracles – or so it would seem to your current consciousness. Are you ready?

*See **Say "Yes" to Love, God Unveils SoulMate Love and Sacred Sexuality.**

I want you to see
how we must move together –
with what grace
and what dedication to serving Love.
I will send you forth to serve Love
in every dimension
and in every stratum of this one.

Becoming the Will of God.
Seeing as God Sees

I am lifting you. I am gently touching you so
that you can feel how everything supports you in Love,
cradles you as Me, loves you, guards and directs you.
Feel how your every moment is this perfect glorious
harmony, perfect Love. This is the future I want you to
actualize. Take this moment – any of these moments
where the truth breaks through as a feeling, and hold it
in your consciousness. Remember it. Cherish it. Bring
it forth into your song of gratitude. Thus every
moment your consciousness will be living in Me, in the
remembrance of your natural state.

It is this state that I come to talk to you about
— this state of beauty and absolute perfection, of joy,
and of Love. Beloved ones, this is the natural extension
of the gratitude experience. Gratitude begins a real
change in consciousness. It moves naturally into action
which is giving and this action starts the flow. It is the
flow of life, of participating in the larger body that
some have called the body of Christ. It is, essentially,
becoming a part of the living expression of My Love
and allowing it to move in you as gratitude and through
you as Love.

In this you are fed — fed the real food of the
living spirit, the food that brings your true self to life.
Oh, dear ones, this movement in your life of

gratitude and giving brings with it a natural elevation of consciousness. It does so because now you have My Love pouring through you. My Love is contacted by your singing gratitude to Me, and pulled through you as you release it forth to bless and heal humanity.

Here then is what must happen next. I know that I am growing you quickly and it seems to your little mind that I am piling up new ideas and attitudes. But don't be fooled. Even this is Old World thinking because you already know all of this. All I am doing is jogging your memory. All I am doing is peeling away the illusion, the old layers of mis-belief and of dis-belief. As I do, precious ones, you will rise up like a flower in the light for this is your natural state. This other state of limitation is put upon you by this world. You who are My "first wave" came specifically to do this — to brush away the illusion and to remember, thus establishing the pattern for all My other children to follow. Yes, there are special young people also awakening, whom you are calling the Indigo Children, but they have a different work. Yours is to set the stage for the mass awakening. The younger ones will verify. They will, essentially, push from behind while you will pull from in front. Together you will hold My beloved humanity in a close embrace, an embrace of loving consciousness, until they, too, understand.

Now I do hold up for you the next step in Christ consciousness, the next step across the divide. You have prayed to Me to see the others, those still lost in the sea of illusion, to see them truly, purely — to be the hollow reed. Some of you have approached Mary to change your vision. You have wondered if she will teach you, will give to you her blessed consciousness of loving My children so perfectly. She is so beautiful! All the heavens are now her robe of glory. Her gentle hand now caresses the entire world. Upon her is the mantle of the Divine Feminine in its purity. And, yes, this is your lineage, those of you who are of feminine charge. Yet even this is not enough.

What? You say this with great surprise. Yet she is here beside you now, assisting the delivery of this new birth within. Precious children, you are My heart. How often I've told you this and how little you can yet understand what this means. Yet even with your limited consciousness, you are growing exponentially. Every day I open you that your spiritual eyes may see the world. Every day I open My heart further that you are stretched to fullest capacity. Oh, a little more! A little more! Each day I deepen your experience of truth — each day then moving beyond Time's influence a little more. *So I now say to you that it is My consciousness that I ask you to claim.*

Silence while you take this in. Yes, I am asking that you think as My consciousness, for it certainly lives within you. I am asking that you now begin to feel as My heart.

Stop! Right there. Let go. Let go of definitions of what this means. Here, beloved ones, is the key. Remember how I told you that gratitude would be your bridge? It is your bridge to everything, to the truth of your real estate, to the real world of a loving heart of God. In gratitude you turn to Me and become the singing joy of gratefulness. *In gratitude there is true humility, for humility is a tenderness of spirit as it turns in faith to Me.* Please let this touch your consciousness. Let yourself remember. Remember our true relationship. Our relationship is a trusting Love, one in which you give yourselves completely to My care. It is rejoicing in the perfection of All I Am, of All I become as I manifest in your life and as I manifest as your life. It is a sweet surrender of exquisite, fulfilling happiness. It is what is right and perfect as your world.

Now dear ones, My consciousness. It is only as you become your true identity that you will be holding the correct consciousness as you love and serve humanity. You have understood that you will have to make a *shift. The shift is seeing humankind as I see and seeing yourselves in service to them.*

This is a very delicate, even dangerous, point. I say this to keep you alert. It is right here that so many beloved ones fall — fall into the precipice of ego. What I tell you next will show you why. It is time for you to serve humanity with all you are — with all your heart and all your spirit, and to love your neighbor as yourself. What does this mean? It means that you must become ego-less. You must see only as I see. You must love your neighbor (all humankind) as your spiritual true God self. Only. You must come to see only this truth as you look at them. You must come to see only as I see.

If you do not make the shift HERE (and I do write it in capital letters), your ego will convince you that you are loving as I love, seeing as I see. Before you know it, you will have a "following." Yes, you could do a lot of good, for you have all learned a lot from Me. But you would fall eventually, for that would be the ego's goal, of course. As is anything created in the World of Old, your good would come and it would fade.

So here you stand, ready for the keys and asking for this shift in consciousness. So I come. Close, close, closer than ever. I now say this to you. If you want this, you can have it. I will give it to you. I will give you the true consciousness, the right attitude. Yet in order to have it truly, you must totally give your life to Me. You must lay it down, **NEVER** to take it up again. *You must live My Will and breathe My Will, eat My Will, sleep My Will. You must softly give your total self and I will lift you into My consciousness. I will show you what it means to be My heart.*

Then dear ones, you will think as Me. You will see as Me, and you will love as Me. Then, dear ones, I will reach as you to tenderly love and bless My own.

Thus I now give you the truth of this. You are to remember your greatest truth, which always must come back to Me. Yet, beloved ones, this too must be easy. It must be a gift of Love, as you give yourselves to Me. There is no time frame. No "shoulds."

Everything is NOW, anyway. Just know where you are going. Me. Nothing less. Believe Me when I tell you that I can show you your heritage. Divine Feminine. Divine Masculine. My own heart. I ask you to remember those beings that you love, who shine their lights on your homecoming path. They are your sisters and brothers of heart. They are the actively "on" cells of My heart. You are still barely awake. Yet as you wake, you are ever their equal. Make no mistake about this, for you can even tarry there – absorbed in those who have come before you – and thus forget that you are already a living part of Me.

Your beloved eyes must always be on Me — not on Mary or on Jesus, on angels or devas, or beings of light from far away. Where your attention is, is where you are going, and as lovely as these beings are, they are not your goal. *The goal is Me. The All in All. The Love That Is. The perfect heart which beats in you in rhythm with all Creation's heart.*

Enjoy your friends, of course! Share your exciting discoveries. Then turn your blessed consciousness to Me to come to claim your true heritage. You are the heart of All That Is. You are this all-consuming Love. You are the All – you. You, beloved ones, can reach in Love through Nature to touch a precious human's face. You can love so vibrantly that simply by seeing your face, one of My precious children will discover who they are. One look as My eyes, one touch as My hands, and you can and will change everything.

Oh, it is no little thing I ask. But I will tell you

that, truly, nothing can be easier. Give yourselves to Me. Then, look into your SoulMate's eyes. You will see yourself. You will know, dear ones, who you are, way beyond ego. In this purity of giving yourself, of laying down your life, you truly will find your life.

Let Me explain this experience. ***It is the recognition, beloved precious tender hearts, that I Am All There Is.*** Seeing Me. Feeling Me. Feeling Me as Love, wrapping you in sweet, sweet tenderness. Gifting you with a surety of Love's reality that nothing can possibly shake. Into this moment of complete perfection, as Nature blesses and all life affirms, comes your Will to give your Will to Me. As you do this, you will feel My Love as gentle arms wrapping you, lifting you into Me in a joy of belonging you have ever been waiting for. In this sweet womb of Love, you then remember that you are twins, that there is another heart that beats with yours. You remember that this glorious Love in which you float is personal. You feel the other. You hear their heart, and you know the comfort of continual, encircling, and mirroring Love. You say, "Yes." "Yes" to this Love as your only truth, your continual reality. All Heaven and Earth witness and concur, as if waves of sweet applause sing forth around you. All you are is My Love, in My Love, and with My Love. Then you know. This other being who shares this womb of Love – this is your SoulMate! And you know, in that instant, that your SoulMate loves you as I do. Completely. Perfectly. Oh, exuberantly! With passion. You know that your heart always has another heart beating with it. You know that the entire universe is yours to love together. You know that being with your

SoulMate, your twin in the womb of Love, your joined truth as a cell of My heart, you will always know My Love. Personally and forever.

When you return to your post, here on Earth, in this continual moment, you will know how it is I see you. You will know how it is that your Love is ever shared, held up around you. How My Love is so perfect, so lavish, so caring, that I would ever give you the company of that Love to manifest, to reflect to you My Love.

Then, beloveds, you will look upon the world and you will only see the good. You will only see My world for you will know Me. You will know how much I love you. You will know how very much I give to you continual experience of that Love and nothing will ever fool you again.

Dear ones, you will look at every human being, then, as I see them. Only good. Only the Christ child standing before you. You will share this outlook with your SoulMate, so together you will hold only the vision of the truth. Now here is where you may ask for your friend, Mary, to assist you, for she can show you the perfect pattern of holding the truth, as she did. Here other beings of light can re-affirm your vision, adding their own experiences. But *you will see with the mind of Christ, for Christ is the truth of humanity as you are in My heart.*

You can practice seeing as I see. But the shift will come when you fully give yourself to Me. When you understand yourselves as My loving heart, having experienced it as My Will for you, then you will truly grasp what any of this means.

Oh, beloved ones, trust that I love perfectly through you. Then listen and watch. You will begin to see it. You will see the New come forth out of the Old. In light. First, perhaps, the outline of each person's truth. Then the entirety – poured out before you in a timeless instant. So you will never again be reinforcing the old, the truth of the separated world. Only the truth of the Christ child within each person. Sleeping within perhaps, but within nonetheless. *You will only love as I love. You will stand before each of My children as Me and see them as I see them.* No matter what, you will then be creating their truth. They will be changed by it. And as you allow My Will, as you see with My vision and love as My heart, if they, for one moment, recognize themselves in your eyes they will be forever changed.

Gratitude is your eyes ever on Me. Giving is the food of the living, moving Love coming through you. Then, as you sing gratitude, as you become the river of moving Love, you will release your Will to Mine and make the leap. From that moment on I will be living through you. From that very moment, you will see the New World – everywhere, in everything.

Dear ones, you may practice seeing as I see, as you continue to give over your Will. It will build an energy that will assist you with the leap or shift. But know that when it happens, it will be easy. You will not have to struggle free of the ever-evaluating ego mind.

You will simply become the mind of Christ. Right now it is a roller coaster – a moment of true consciousness, many moments in the little mind. Remember that where your attention is, is everything. Thus, dear ones, just look at Me. Look at Love as it manifests as your SoulMate. Do not waver, and you will build up "frequency," as you call it, until you change worlds.

Thus it makes sense to practice, dear ones – to practice loving as I love, seeing as I see, remembering who your SoulMate really is, and acting as if you live in Love's full reality.

Now that you know your purpose and your truth, you know why I am pushing you, loving you passionately. You know why I am lifting you up until you are close enough to see only Me. Then you will be ready to serve the world as My Love, My hands, and My heart. Always.

Surrender into Love.
Surrender into Love for Me.
That IS Christ consciousness.
For what is Christ?
My living Love.
What are you?
Love's vehicle.

Becoming the River of Love.
The Ascension Happens Naturally

I am Love, and I come to claim you. I am life, and I come to live you. I am joy and I come to dance upon the waters of Creation as your heart. When you have given your Will to Me, you have allowed Me to come ever and ever more fully into your life. It is this sweet obedience that brings you up into My arms, and brings Me to dwell within you.

Dear ones, I show you now what we are becoming. In doing this, I set the stage for all who are ready to "hand over" their life. I want to show you that Love is the law. There is no other. Only by Love, only by becoming My Love can you be free to rise in the ascension. Of yourselves, in your little minds, you cannot accomplish this. Not ever. As I show you our transformation, you will also come to see that even here there is another "dispensation." You will see that the Violet Flame is not enough, for even as you use it, so you see yourselves as needing its assistance. So, in all your plans, in your dreams of overcoming, you must come to a new understanding.

This understanding is Love as your focus, yes. But only in the surrender of your life to Me can real Love become your identity. I must love My children through you. I must become your hands and your heart. Even then, you must continually ask Me to dissolve your little Will into Mine.

First, there is your SoulMate — the gift of living Love before you, to show you every moment if you are giving Love. Then there is the process of dissolving, where together you become one heart. That heart must then become My own. As it does, I will come to you. I will take up residence within, for remember, I am in everything, including within you. Yet even with this, you must stretch yourselves, that your heart can be large enough to do My Will.

Beloved ones, there is tenderness for every single point of life, every being who is alive, for all are alive in Me. How can I convey this except to say that you must want it? You must want to become My living Love. My living presence as your heart. You must want it enough to really give your life to Me. When you do, it does not matter where it goes. It does not matter if you are "ascending," if you are "on the path," or "up the mountain." All that matters is Love and allowing My Will to live you, to teach you, to show you what it is to become My Love, being given as you.

As you come ever closer, as you open in joy and in ecstasy, you will find a grace that is the real living food of divine Love moving through you from Me. Beloved ones, this grace will lift you perfectly. This Love will wash away your past. It will simply remove any unbalanced energies. It will transform every increment of karma, and it will do it automatically – as Love is given. As Love goes out from you, so Love is drawn in. And, beloved ones, if you have given Me your Will, then this Love will be increasing every single moment. The more clearly you are Mine, the more open you will be. The higher will be the sparkling river of Love as it is given through you every moment.

You will feel this Love as everything you are. You will be amazed at how deeply you can feel, how expansive your desire to love. You will be amazed at how great your capacity, as you become My flowing river of sparkling, dancing, blessing, glorious Love.

Every moment I will fill you. I will pour you out upon My children. And every moment all it takes is for you to turn over your little Will and to will to be My Love. To give your entirety to Me. To allow Me to become your living presence – your life, your breath, your everything.

Then I will bathe you in the river of our giving, living Love and you will feel the tenderness. Oh, how you will feel the Love of My precious humanity. How you will feel the honor of serving them. This tenderness is your obedience lifting you up as My awakened heart.

Oh, beloved ones, Love will then be all you are. Love will live you, for this is My Will, and in living you, it will give you. It will give you to the "least" as well as the "best" of humanity. It will give you to Nature for its blessing and healing. It will give you, of course, to the communion of Love that is the awakened cell of you and your SoulMate. And in the giving of you, you will be freed.

So, as always, take no thought of your little self – even of your ascension in the light. Beloved ones, even this thought holds within it your un-ascended self. In this thought you are saying, "I'm not there yet. I need to be more – more of this, more of that. More Violet Flame, a percentage of light…" and all the while you are creating the continuation of your un-ascended state.

Oh, precious ones, you cannot get there with your little Will, for giving is the only route. In giving, you become the heart of Love that you are in truth. In giving your Will I can return you to your perfection. Giving your Will that we become one. Forever. It is this oneness that is the ascension, and it is the river of living Love that is the key. This Love, when moving through you enough – fast enough, fully enough – as you give and give and give, it will transform you as you look at Me. As you give your Will and you become the river of giving Love, you become your true or "higher" self. You become Love.

Oh, blessed ones, this Love that I Am, that I seek now to give to the world in and through you – it is a sparkling river of the substance of life in its true intention of My Will. Oh, as it grows from a trickling stream that is moving from you to the heart of your SoulMate, to a glorious river, a flood of life, it will transform you instantly. It will return you to your perfection. It will lift you into our fullest partnership. In that moment, when you are the whole river by obedience to Love (whose nature is giving, forever), you are "washed clean." Every single electron of every part of you is cleansed and filled with Love. *Everything you have ever carried that was less than Love is gone.*

There is then nothing in you but Love. Your mind is on Love. Your heart is in Love. Your attention is ever on giving Love forth. You have Love before you as your SoulMate (by this point, guaranteed). Your Will is Love in Me. So, Love, dear ones, is all you see, within you and without. All your karma is erased. All misqualified energy transformed. In that moment, you are Love. in every cell and every atom for all eternity. Then, without ever having "tried" for it, you will be ascended — free forever, across the divide, beyond death or limitation.

So can you see that it is in our joining that this becomes possible? If you give Me your Will, if you ask Me to love as you, to give Love through you, then you are co-creating our union. You are creating the giving of Love in yourself. If, instead, you are seeking to "will yourself" free, your attention is given to your own little world. This river of giving, the flow of All That Is, is not started in you. Working for your own ascension is like forever dividing numbers in half: There will always be more to "divide," more things to conquer. There will always be more Violet Flame needed – because this is the focus of your co-creative consciousness. .

Beloved ones, I promise you, you cannot do this of yourself. The only way is our communion, the giving of even your very own Will. Otherwise the little will or ego has an entry point – your focus on yourself, and you can see your co-creative abilities will ever be creating more to overcome.

I will come to live in you. Remember how Jesus, who is your example, was always saying this? "Of myself, I do nothing. The Father within me doeth the works." Whatever you name Me, I am waiting for you. I am waiting to take up residence as the power and the presence of your heart. Then I will teach you perfectly (for I will not come until you give Me your Will). Every moment I will open you more and more to this river of Love. I will grow in you the Will to give, and I will open in you My own tenderness. Then, when you see any of My humanity, your heart will rush to open, to give them access through you — access to My precious, flowing river of Love. Access to the hope of this eternal reality. Oh, you will feel the great desire to hold them in it, to embrace them with it, to wrap them in a blanket of Love.

And, oh, the compassion in your every encounter. You will rush toward them in tender solicitation, for, oh, how you suffer to see them lost. You can't wait to relieve them of the darkness they live in. You will remember, for your heart will read instantly the terrible reality at the mercy of their ego. You will remember how it is to be shaken by fear, locked in the jaws of depression, tossed like a rag doll on the currents of darkness, never knowing what you will feel from one moment to the next. Oh, My beloved children, I never dreamed you would live thus. And you who are hearing Me, can you answer this great need to love them as My own comforter, as you live in the world?

Then, as you know My tenderness and you also have experienced even a little of the glory of the river of giving, moving Love, this will become all that matters to you. So you will seek to open ever further and further to My Will that this river of Love can flow through you ever more freely, fully, in great torrents of blessing for this parched world. You will see, then, the results as the darkness is dissolved, as this flood of Love is poured upon it. Everything it touches will respond. It is the truth of My being, and thus of yours, in ways you cannot comprehend.

Then, beloved ones, as you tenderly feed the drooping spirits of My children, as you become the living Love that I pour into their hearts, you truly will know that this is all. All there is. All you need. All you have ever cared to do or be. You will become, as Jesus did, the living Christ, which is My Love poured forth as you, forever.

Dear ones, using Jesus again, for such is the purpose of his life (far beyond any religion, of course), his "temptation" in the desert was exactly this — that he focus on himself in his spiritual growth. It is translated in the Bible as the temptation of worldly kingdoms. It was the temptation to become a great spiritual adept and thus to have not only Earth, but all the worlds of all the universes bow to him. It would have meant to be his fullness as a cell in My heart, but to focus all the energy into himself. And, beloved ones, just as it is for you, it was very hard for him to distinguish. Wasn't the point of this incarnation to show humanity a spiritual adept? A person who has become their fullest potential? Of course it is, he thought.

He could have done it easily, for he had access to all power through his awakened heart. But he realized, as he prayed and prayed, that it meant taking his Will back out of Mine. And when he understood, he also realized that I would only give, never get, and so he understood. He chose this very river of giving, and he became the living Christ. He did not need to go through such temptation – he had to agree to be separated from Me for a while - but he did it, as with everything he did, to lay before you the truth of this path you are on.

So as you grow into Me, as you give your Will over to Mine, you will find yourself longing for this river of Love. You will long to feel this divine Love. To be it. To free it in My children.

It is to this that I have brought you, step by careful step, through the loving of your SoulMate, that you might see what it is to feel this Love move through you, and that you can recognize yourself in their eyes of shining Love.

I have brought you close through gratitude, tuning you to giving forth. I have been tuning your hearts very carefully. I have trained your minds to lift to Me. To serve for Me, and then to give to Me everything — your very perceptions of the world (to move beyond evaluating, to become the hollow reed).

At last I move within you, that the shining star within your chest, the heart of Love you become with your SoulMate, your very breath, your prayers, your every moment, including every cell of your physical body

ARE MINE. Mine to love through, to live through, to speak through, and to bless.

And though you have barely touched a tiny stream, you have experienced this river of Love. You have been lifted in ecstasy; touched with the light, felt the first movement of perfect Love through you. I am training you carefully. Then I have brought you back down into the old world of fear and depression, so you could understand the tenderness. So that you could remember how awful it is to be at the mercy of these clouds of feeling, to be rocked and buffeted by emotional storms. To know what it feels like to never know what will become of you one moment to the next.

I do this to be sure that every time you look upon your fellow humans you will be longing to bring Me through to them. To see every one, oh, with such compassion! To rush to give them every possible assistance. Every ray of hope, every tiny relief. To be at service to Love continually. You will never again see them from your own Will or ego, beloveds, but only as Me, as I Am in you as I Am Love waiting to live you, to pour through you.

Once you come to know this river of giving Love (which is what I Am, at levels you cannot begin to dream), you will know. You will know that even a trickle of this water of Love, this substance of life, will erase the darkness. It cannot do otherwise. So even if you deliver only a tiny amount, you could have just erased a lifetime of karma. You will come to see this life-giving water. You will come to see its effects. As you allow Me to use you, as together we love humanity, you will see it transform the dull gray that surrounds My children to the sparkling transparency of Love's living light. If you enjoy gardening, it is as if all of these precious children are like little plants trying to grow in the dark for the lie of illusion, the terrible clouds of the ego, keep My nurturing light from ever getting near them.

Yes, ultimately each must say "yes" to Love on his or her own in order to begin a true spiritual awakening. But, oh, you can help, My beloved ones, so much! You can remove the inky darkness with the washing in this water of Love. Then, of course, they'll be able to see, to get a glimpse, to sense something that speaks to the spirit in them. A spark, a jolt, and we're on our way. But until they can respond, they are lost in that night.

Sparkling, living, giving Love! Bathe yourselves in it truly, as you create the flow by your higher Will. Your Will as Mine, your Will to love. To love, to give, to love, to give. You can look up to this from where you are and begin to bring it through your life. But more perfectly, just will to give your own sweet Will to Me, for then you are living the higher life and I will grow you perfectly. "Prime the pump" with your SoulMate, with loving them with all you are. But even there you will reach a point that to continue to go higher, you must give your Will to Me.

You cannot yet even conceive, beloved ones, of the rushing Love of this sparkling glory of cascading grace that washes everything it lifts in its currents. So of course, as you give it, so you are given Love into ever greater Love —greater Love and greater Love, lighting you far beyond yourself, until washed clean in its currents as it flows outward from you, you become this moving Love itself. Then you are free, beloved ones. This is what you name the ascension. You will get there by giving, only, by letting go of yourself to find yourself, to be reborn as the Love that you really are.

Trust in this process. Your heart will verify it for you. The moment you experience the true giving of Love, you will know that I would only ever design it like this. You will know that by giving yourself to the giving of Love, you are lifted from your little world to Mine. Giving Love is all that I am, so in it, of course, you will find yourself.

Open yourself to this glorious Love. One touch and you will know its truth as who you are, as what I am. You will know it is the answer to bringing humanity home.

Oh, dear ones,
to those of you who do know
this great Love
and who rest in it,
this is My call to you.
Every true light must go forth
to do My Will quickly.

Moving Into the New World Now

I truly hold you cupped within My hands. I hold you with great, great tenderness, living within My heart. This, dear ones, is the truth of it.

A new door is opening. It will be one that will be for all of you to anticipate. It begins a shift that will bring you through the veil. I am now beginning to teach you how to bring the New World fully through. Fully into manifestation here in your hearts and in your consciousness. I will open the door carefully. At first it will be beyond the reach of your ordinary mind. But it will never be beyond the reach of your hearts.

Oh, yes, I will pour this vision through. I will wrap you in it. I will lift you to it. I will continue to reveal it to each of you. Because each of you hears and sees differently, because each of you has different areas where you are most clear, together you will share in the building of this. Each of you will understand first one piece, then another, until with rising joy and ecstasy you come to live in fullness in the world of truth.

I must lay a foundation. Until now, you have believed that you are physical beings, living each day in a physical world. Oh, I do not mean that you don't understand your spiritual nature, for you do, or I would certainly never be presenting what I am. But you have been willing to believe that the world is "defined" — that laws of gravity and of functioning, of health and anatomy, and the existence of the soil, the trees, the Earth herself, have a recognized solidity.

It is time for this to change. It is time, dear ones, for you to shift from being here looking toward the New World to being in the New World, looking back upon the old.

Beloved ones, your consciousness has now progressed sufficiently for you to accept and begin to live what I have prepared for you. Very carefully, through all the years you have each been on Earth this time, every increment of opening, every communion with Nature, every conviction of this greater truth, every deep communion with My presence, has been stored up for you. You have heard the phrase, "Lay up your treasures in heaven"? This is exactly what we have been doing. Together we have all agreed that this time would come and this place would be ready. Just so you know, beloved ones, you yourselves have been here before, preparing the energy and creating this focus. Certainly each of you is aware that wherever you are, there is something truly amazing there. Oh, yes, there is beauty, so very necessary to nourish you, but there is more. There is no need for details, for this must not ever be about the little mind and how it loves to search the past and build convoluted mazes that are there to pull your attention to it.

No, all that matters here are your hearts. Though you are still learning things, in essence you are ready. You are ready to begin this process of spiritualizing your very body, of living every moment by choice, and that choice always Me. You are ready to lift your little Will into My greater one, that I may give you back your perfected self when you have fully succeeded.

It is time to choose the New World — to "act as if," as you say. It is time to live and move and have your being in the glorious expansiveness. It is time, dear ones, to place your precious vision totally on perfection. It is time to know the truth of Oneness, and understanding this in fullness, you will be My heart manifest in the world.

No more looking at yourselves as being "on your way." No more seeing anything less than perfect Love and perfect peace – and perfect glory. Truly I do come to paint before you the wonder of your hearts. Do you see it? Do you see the beauty manifest? Do you see the singing, sweet and holy harmony? Oh, if you do not, then come outside and look. Look. Feel the vibration. You will know. You will know that I Am. You will know not only are we one, but so is everything. There is only Me. Only us. Only Love. Only beauty, perfection, peace and the amazing song of Creation in which I sing forth in the ecstatic expression of My being.

I know you have read or heard such things — God is One. All is God. God is all there is. All who are ready will now experience this. You will experience this truth of Love with trillions of parts. This song of Creation in "billion-part harmony." This truth of your beings that All I Am, you are also. Thus All That Is, is alive in you.

At first, for a little while, you will still see

yourselves as having experiences. You will experience yourself being honored, yourself in communion. And as yet, this part is still necessary. But as you continue to truly bask in the truth of the New, to choose to see it, to live it, to call it ever fully into your consciousness, here is what is happening.

These hearts of yours, that you currently identify? Beloved ones, your entire being is a heart! Remember? You are, together in your SoulMate union, a cell of My heart. What does this mean? It means that as your light is switched on, as your Love comes pouring through the two of you together, *every cell in your body, every particle of your larger selves, will recognize itself as Love. This, dear ones, is what it means to live in Love. Then as you embrace the truth of Love, the truth of your beings and the truth of the New World, what you now feel in your hearts will then pour through your entire being.* Oh, as it does, beloved ones, you then become what you truly are — that switched on cell of My great heart.

Since Love is the substance of All That Is, then All That Is will be as One with you. There truly is no way as yet to bring this through to you. Suffice it to say you will be in Love with All That Is. You will be All That Is. Yet you will also be you, perfectly, for it is your highest fulfillment to be your perfection, together, in the joyous oneness and yet perfect individuality.

You can begin this shift. You are ready. And if you place this awareness within, you will know it is correct. You have come to the point where you are as far as you can go by "being here" and looking "over there," still seeing yourselves as unperfected, "fallen" humans who are growing.   So now I give to each of you this shining vision of perfection. *I place you here, beloved ones, where by your own preparation and your diligent evolution, by your Love and your commitments, by your loving SoulMate consciousness, by all of this and by our communion lifting you daily in unity, the veil is very thin.*

In truth, this means that the heaven worlds, the higher realms are here. Here, manifest in unity, whenever you are ready. Whenever you take the scales from your eyes. Whenever you remove all fear from your hearts. Whenever you are ready to recognize Me in everything, then you will exist in the New. Right here. Yes, you have known this. As a future. *I ask you to choose it as a Now.*

You have all had moments of this experience, where you have known the perfection. You have all seen before you the shimmering vision of the glorious truth – that what you are seeing is just the faintest beginning of the absolute magnificence of the Real World, the world that you are to claim.

As you are successful in your continual experience, beloved ones, as you move ever more fully into the New World here, those beings who occupy the higher vibrations will become ever more real to you. *This is a process in which you agreed to participate – that you will create this haven of the New yet remain connected to the Old World reality, that you may*

bring humanity Home with you. So you will exist "between the worlds," able to see both and to function in both, too. ***Dear ones, you will be residing here in the perfect New, yet you will be able to turn and reach back through the veil at Will, to serve and to promote the recognition of Love and perfection and ecstasy.***

This is why I have been training you intensely through these Messages. This is what I am growing you into. Yet in this phase of your shifting consciousness, it will be up to you to act "as if" continually. As you certainly know by now, where your attention is, is what you create. Thus your attention must now shift into claiming the New World as your reality.

Any last experiences of ego you may have are to solidify your decision to ever change your consciousness. You can see nothing as outside of Me and thus nothing as outside yourselves. You must see right through any and every possible story the ego will present to you. Beloved ones, that is the only thing that will bring you back into the false reality, back into a world of separation, back where you cannot do your joy of lifting My humanity, for what you see is what you energize. What you believe, you create, including every explanation. Every one, dear ones. This includes believing in cellular memory, past experiences, emotional trauma, or being repulsed by bad manners or ignorance or any false definition of reality.

Every one, including you, is Me. God. Beauty. Oh, every precious one of you is absolutely beyond belief (held currently). If you see anything else, you have lost your footing in the New. Yes, when you look you can acknowledge if I am hidden or I am recognized. However, it is obvious that in any who are living in the Old, I will be hidden. You must find Me. Remember that I have said that you must look straight through the illusion? Straight through, precious ones.

This is why you who are reading these Messages are training in the world each day with precious ones who are sleeping, in whom I am hidden. In these beings, the seed of Me needs nurturing to even catch their notice. Later, as I bring you into contact with those who are searching, dear ones — if there is any lie within you, any hooks, any false belief, they will catch you. Why? Because those who are searching are closer to your reality. It will be more enticing to believe, more places for those ego hooks. Do you not believe Me? Do you think it will be obvious, who is who and what is what? Let Me tell you that it will not. There will be "signs and wonders." There will be magnificent demonstrations by the anti-Christ, who is, of course, not a being but an energy that your little mind will use to keep you hooked.

You must be so fully in My Will that nothing else can interest you — including false roads to ecstasy as well as sad tales of personal ego, yours or others.

Thus, as you now choose to live the New, to take up residence in Love, our goal is that everything will change. Every encounter you have will occur while you are reaching back through the veil to assist in the blessing and healing and uplifting of the world. Can you see how this changes everything? How you will ever be centered in the truth of Love? How the pageantry of ego before you will mean nothing – that all that matters is the delivery of Love? *It will mean the finding of My face within them.* The affirmation, through your attention, of the Christ in them. If you do this successfully, they will see themselves. They will notice your perfect positive regard. Right then you have claimed their heart for Me.

Of course, even anti-Love isn't real. And the moment Love is seen as truth, the only truth, the illusion must begin to fade, until truth after truth, the New World comes forth, *born of human attention to Love.*

Thus you must be solid in your own commitments – to ever see only Love. Every acknowledgment of the opposite, in even the smallest way, keeps those precious cells of My very own heart turned off and keeps the world lost in the mist.

As you focus on the New World, you will bring it forth. You haven't seen how big you are or the truth of your reality as My heart. But you are getting glimpses. You each have moments in the New – moments when you become Love, where you are the consciousness of unity. In those moments, you are embraced as All That Is Real reflects to you your truth.

Everything is an expression of My Love. Thus *everything meeting anything else truly is Me greeting Myself. Love caressing Love.* In any moment where you make it through, you will find yourself singing in great harmony with all the expressions of what I Am all around you. It is a huge, glorious song of everlasting communion. And when your attention is drawn to any one part, then you sing a little duet with that piece of My being

Oh, it is true that words are very pale in comparison. So, dear ones, is everything you think you know. Every definition – of tree, of wind, of sunset or rainbow. Every experience of color, of life force. As you look out on this beauty before you, I ask you to look carefully, in complete inner communion of Love with all you see. Then look even harder. Even strain to see the real expression of all before you. It will begin to break through, for you are claiming it. You are drawing it forth by your attention and your Love. You will catch the shimmering, the iridescence of the colors beyond anything you've ever seen. You will also begin to have a new inner landscape far more filled with beauty and overflowing, effervescent joy.

Yet knowing this, this joy in sweet communion, you must know also that each of you is performing a unique service – that of being open to both worlds, that you may bring the others Home. You have always known this but now there is a difference. Up until now, you too were looking up from within the illusion in the experience of the Old (which will and must pass away). You are now to hold the anchor from the New and pull the others to you.

So your goal in everything is choice – choice to love and to live in the New while, with oh, the greatest tenderness, reaching back to hold impeccably

the recognition of Me in each person, no matter what their ego says. You will have no ego to respond to the waving flags of falsity. Do you see? If you live purely, embracing Love - held sweetly in Creation - everything around you will be drawn to express the highest good. This automatically brings you into right relationship with every heart in your vicinity.

So essentially we are forming a greeting station and you are to be the welcoming committee from the New, presenting to humanity an ever-clearer glimpse of their perfection.

You will be serving all, dear ones, down every strata of the illusion, and you will see every one in Love and speak the truth for them to hear. The more firmly that you live the New, the more clearly you will see the truth beneath every idea everyone has of themselves – for this is of course what is manifesting.

I will continue to open your hearts and establish your vision in the truth of the New. Oh, beloved ones, we have such a glorious, never-ending expression of Love to explore together. Take a leap!

*I ask you to
go to your heart
and to feel how much I love
every human being.
Each one is so precious,
so beautiful,
so amazing and unique.
The heart seeks only to show them this,
to give to them
the Love that is their heritage.*

Our Heart's Desire

I am Love. I am the sun, kissing your face with warmth. I am the sweet breeze caressing your skin. I am the cradle of stars that hold you in their midst. I am the great cosmos, of which you are the center. I am Love, and you, My beloved precious children – you are Me in Love with life.

What does this mean? It means that you are My heart living in experience. You are My Love pressed up against the world. You are the living moving motion of Love, touching life from moment to moment to moment. Touching life, yes. Touching life and finding it good.

Finding life good. Beloved ones, this is My decree. This is what is ever meant to be the heart of My experience. As I sang forth My glory, sending those stars and worlds winging on their courses, it was My expression of glory. My expression of greatest joy, of pure exquisite ecstasy. It was the bursting forth of My Love because I was so much Love, that I had to share. I had to give. From this singing celebration came everything — All That Is, the vastness and the complexity of which are currently beyond your consciousness.

You are My heart alive in experience. You are the center of the vastness. You!

What does it mean to be My Love in experience? Beloved ones, it is simply and profoundly that you are My Love in motion, the energy of life, of All, as I pour forth My desire that Love be experience. You are the emotion of God. Emotion, as I have often told you, is energy in motion. It is the glorious movement of Love as it reaches out to love itself as everything. *Thus are you Love's passionate experience as, in wonder, it becomes ever more, ever new.*

Oh, beloved ones, you are My heart in motion, in experience. Thus, dear ones, *what is the creative force of all experience? It is your heart's desire.*

I have been teaching you about the power of thought, about thought as the mold that becomes filled with your Love. It is very important. But, beloved ones, *way beyond thought is the power of your emotion.* First you must learn how to return your attention. You must learn to clear out the effluvia of the lie. You must come to still the mind, to bring it back into position as that which is ever in service to the heart. I have spoken of your heart in many ways. From the moment we began this shift, I said that you had to switch from the ego to the heart as your place of experience, the point of your consciousness.

Then I have explained to you a greater, more magnificent truth. Your heart is larger than a single part. That rather than one, you are two. You are your SoulMate. In doing this, I have returned to you your birthright of Love, the truth of your experience. Every moment you are ever meant to see Love manifested before you. You are meant to experience Love in your life, real beautiful, tender, glowing, growing, manifested Love as you clear your vision and see your SoulMate. This, dear ones, is the truth of Love made manifest. The truth of your heart, and your truth as My heart is a magnificent dance of experience through which Love truly becomes your continual reality.

Now you have given your Will to Me. You have come to be humbled by the magnitude of Love. You have come to understand that it is bigger than your ability to currently understand. So you have placed your Will in Mine. You have given Me your Love that I may give it back to you, multiplied, magnified into the greater Love I Am. Doing this, you have cleared your mind, essentially saying to Me, "God, even in this we know there is far more than we can see. What would you have living within us?"

So I come, oh precious ones, in jubilation – oh, at last! I come to give you the greatest gifts — the truth of the power of your heart. All the while you have been turned from Me, dreaming dreams of negativity, I have continually held you alive in Me and whispered the truth — *anything your heart desires, you will have.* Anything your heart desires. Beloved ones, what is desire? It is emotion. It is the energy of Love in motion. Well, you are Love (whether you are aware of it or not). You are part of My heart, and your heart is a perfect reflection of this. Your heart is the center of your being. It is the energy center. It is what is vitalized.

You know, all of you, about your heart. *What you haven't quite understood is the power of your heart's desires. Your heart's desires are the emotions that are alive in the center of your being.* Your heart's desires are the emotions that you have stored in your heart, held deep in the center of your being. These desires are emotions that are meant to be My experience of life here, in you, as you, in all your planes of existence. These emotions, of course, were always meant to be the experience of Love joyfully moving forth as life.

However, because you accept the belief of negativity here in this place of "good and evil" (the place being your beliefs, of course), oh, beloved ones, what have you stored in your hearts? Fear of Love. This is the biggest one. As I look at My precious humanity, I see hearts that are dark, that look more like walnuts, held in the chests of My children. Dark and hard and closed to Love. *The movement of Love, dear ones, is life. So the glory of My universe, the sweeping currents of ecstasy, the singing choruses of angelic rejoicing, the triumphant bells of the archangels' laughter, the movement of all the fire of life itself, is denied access here.*

Oh, how many of you believe that Love will hurt you? It is almost unbearable to think of, isn't it? No, don't feel it, whatever you do. I give it only so those of you hiding from Love may recognize yourselves.

Oh, precious humanity, if you have any spark of life left in your heart, use every bit of faith and courage to throw off the lie of false desires of the heart because I can promise you that I give you anything you place within your heart.

This is the power of SoulMate Love, of course, as I have told you. Yet even understanding this is only the first step, even the clearing of your mind, even giving Me your Will. *It is only the beginning of giving you back right desire in your heart.*

So, as you learn to fly with Love, as you release your Will to Mine, I will begin to give to you the experience of real emotion. Yes, ecstasy is a very good start. Gratitude is ecstasy's doorway. But, beloved ones, it is true emotion that can rock the heavens and that can power the Earth. It can light and heat your homes. It can shine forth your great and glorious rays of light that are generated by your moving Love in all the ways it feels to you – as the glory of humanity and as the song of eternal life.

When you have stilled your mind and moved into your heart as the center of your existence, when you have cleared away your ego by releasing your Will to Me, then you are ready. It may still be a little while, but I want you to be waiting — waiting for the blending — the blending of our being until you begin to have My experience. Of course, I am within you as well as without and when your little Will is gone and your attention is on Me, you will begin to feel it. True emotion. The energy of Love in motion. You will feel the experience of being the point where I come to touch the world of form and experience that you occupy. You will feel it the moment when the reservoir of your heart becomes My energy in motion.

It may start as only little moments — moments where I reach as you to pour forth as Love upon humanity or on a specific person. It may start as the moment when you know absolutely that I am loving your SoulMate as you. Or the moment when your entire being begins to vibrate in the song of Love and you simply disappear into the experience of Love pouring through your heart. It may come as the moment when your heart is the perfection of communion of Love as the All and Love as the manifest. It is a sweet, high, refined refrain. It is also a gloriously passionate one! It is emotion as I experience it. It is when the desire of our hearts is one.

Oh, at this moment, these may be mainly words, but underneath I promise I have placed the experience so you will begin to prepare for it, so you will become the true desire of Love.

And so, My beloved ones, you will know how to assist the ones who come to you. You can tenderly shine the light of My Love upon the truth of the desires that are held in their heart. You can assist them to see why they are manifesting their fear of Love instead of the glorious Love that is their truth.

I will give you your heart's desire. Just as you recognized the truth of these words immediately, so will others.

You cannot skip the steps. Each of you must

release the false world and turn your attention back to me. You must choose to remember that I am only good, only light, only Love. You must acknowledge your existence as the heart of your being. And each of you, having deeply chosen the truth of Love, will find your consciousness waking to the truth of your SoulMate.

Then, dear ones, you shall release your false identity and place your little Will in the service of My greater Will. Thus freed, you become ready to experience your truth in Me. Your Love becomes My Love poured forth into experience. As you do this, the moment you reach out your hands to touch, at that moment you will truly experience the full truth of that which you are touching.

You will breathe the true nectar of Nature. Yes, this I promise. You will become the experience of Love moving into form. You will, for that moment, have communion with that deva. Should you reach forth to another of My beloved human children, you will experience, in that moment, the truth of his or her being. So as you stand there looking at them you will not see the illusion. You will see as I see. And thus will you give them the greatest of all gifts. You will plant within their human consciousness the truth of their divinity. Once you have done this, beloved ones, the illusion will not hold them much longer – no matter how far it seems they have to go.

Just as you know in the depth of your being, all it takes is one moment of recognition. So in truth all these steps could be the span of one breath, if that was all that was needed. One breath to be free of the illusion. One breath to the recognition of Love. One breath to communion of their heart as their SoulMate. One breath to the giving of their Will. And one more breath to the return to their experience of our union. One more breath to desiring humanity's freedom. And then like spring planting will the truth of each of you be planted, to be nourished by the first of you who are now waking to the truth. Then manifesting your heart's desire is manifesting theirs, and in the space of another moment you have all come Home.

Now is the time of our blended Will — that I may teach you who you are, that I may plant in each of you the remembrance of your heart's desire. Do not make it complicated, for of course this would delight your little minds. It would keep you safely away from the truth to believe that there were hierarchies and initiations and much complicated learning. It is simple, beloved ones. *It is the emotion of your heart that manifests as your reality.* And it is the emotion of your heart, your heart's desire, which will change your life. It is that simple.

Yet you did have to learn (and many still do) that your thoughts are where your attention is. *Your thoughts form beliefs that fuel your emotions that ultimately become the truth of your heart.* How many of you, My beloved ones, believe your heart is broken? Millions of you, beloved ones. Millions. This then becomes your heart's desire, because it is the emotion of your heart – the energy in motion to which you lend your creative power. You are the heart of God, My heart, which in itself should tell you what this means.

First, you must change your mind. This should be obvious to you. Only then can I have access to you, and reconnection to your heart. Any thoughts of negativity (even those not yet a belief) are like insulation, keeping the spark of My life in you away. The veil we speak of continually is exactly this — a great insulation field of negativity that keeps you from the truth.

For those who are ready, you will begin having this experience — this flash of living, moving Love where you disappear into Me. An experience where My Love becomes you meeting My Love as experience. You will recognize it. You will be lifted completely beyond your human consciousness. You will become the emotional experience of My living, moving Love. Watch! Reach for it. Spend as many of your moments as you can in your heart, expectantly. At first it will be flashes of communion, ecstasy, and then beyond anything definable, beyond mind, only true emotion, sacred feeling. Look for this through your communion with each other, SoulMates. And look for this in the places where you feel closest to Me.

Give Me your Will that I can give it back to you. Once you understand the glorious experience of Love living you, then you can take back the naming of your heart's desires. Once your Will is gone to Mine, you will be fed by the joy of giving; the ecstasy of communion with your SoulMate for the freeing of My children. Yet once you have claimed our union of Will, then you can act as Me, beloved ones, in bringing perfection back into view. This is how Jesus did his healings. This is how he loved and fed the multitudes. He saw them as I see them. And this is what I build in you.

This is what I build in you and what I ask you to deliver. I have brought forth the information that Love is All I Am. It has taken root through many different teachings. Now just as with the understanding of Jesus as the way-shower rather than the savior, so must we bring forth the understanding that good is what you are, My entire beloved humanity. Love is what you are. Good is all you see. And the desires of your heart are ever what you manifest. It's really simple, isn't it?

As you pour forth Love, ask Me to show you how it feels. As your spirit rises into wonder and joy, ask Me to show you ecstasy. Just as in all that you are learning, you have no frame of reference, for what you call joy is pale indeed compared to joy in Me. What you name Love, beloved ones, is barely a taste of Love's real substance. Love can feed you and it can build a world, a life, a relationship. Allow Me then to show you how real it is. Allow Me to bring it forth in you. Prepare to be amazed.

"Thy kingdom come, thy Will be done, on Earth as it is in Heaven." Remember who it was who spoke these words. You might want to consider using them. Then wait on Me in expectation. Love will come to claim you, that you will become the desire of a larger heart than the little one you currently see. The heart of Christ is who you are. The heart of Christ is Me.

You see,
Jesus did not always look like the Christ.
But he was.
Every single moment.
For he allowed Me
to do his greater work through him.
It did not look like the
Christ of God upon that cross.
At any moment,
Jesus had the power to work his own Will.
He could have said,
"Well, surely this does not look like
an example of the power of God's light!"
He could have blasted forth
and floated free above that cross.
But he did not.
Why?
Because he gave his Will to Me.
And in doing so,
he saved a world
and proved later that the Christ stood forth
in victory over death.
As was My Will.

Making the Leap. Becoming Only Love As We Give Our Will to God

This is a time in the history of the world where decisions are of great importance. Truly every moment now, the question comes before you — where is your allegiance? Whom do you serve? Yet, that which seemed clear to you even a month ago, even yesterday, now requires a discernment never before required. The fate of the world rests on you.

The fate of the world rests on you, My beloveds of the light who are reading these words, for it is your hearts that have called to Me and offered yourselves. It is your sincerity, your Love, which has brought all humanity to this moment, to these choices. *It is you who have given Me your hearts and lives in service to the raising up of all My beloved children here on Earth.* And, oh, I have taken you up on it! I have altered the natural order of things, that Love might show forth its beauty even here, in the shadow world.

Beloved ones, it is these shadows that I now passionately address for the fate of this shift is on you. It is on you who are awake to Me, you whose beautiful eyes are raised to the higher realms and whose sweet countenances bring the angels to their knees in gratitude.

Yet, if the way had been easy, it would have already been accomplished. Thus, now more than ever,

175

there must be a vigilance of consciousness that is dawning in the world. Beloved, most precious of My heart, that consciousness is this.

The only way to make this shift, to make it across the chasm between the Old World and the New, is to let Me carry you. I tell you simply and truly, there is no way you can do this without Me. Not only without Me in your lives, for all of you have Me. So obviously there is something more. More than looking to Me. More than studying the paths, the words, the consciousness of those who have gone before you. More, beloved ones, even than understanding the beautiful New World, the golden age of Love and peace.

You must come to live here. You must come to lift them up, your brothers and your sisters. You must be able to manifest in you everything I Am. You must become, as Jesus did, the living moving Christ — the heart of Love that sees only Love and can never see anything else. You must become the heart and the consciousness that lives firmly in the truth.

Beloved ones, I call you to this knowledge, to the remembrance of what already lives inside of you. Of yourselves you cannot accomplish this. Of yourselves, you cannot see it clearly enough. You cannot live it powerfully enough to bring all the rest of our beloved ones and all the glorious parts of them back to the perfection. Including this beautiful and precious Earth.

You cannot know from here. You cannot lift from here. You cannot gain the altitude, the clarity, the wonder, the sparkling pristine light of the perfect moving Love. It is not possible. Yet your egos will do all they possibly can to convince you otherwise. Oh, beloved ones, this is why I come with so much passion, so much tenderness. ***The only way you can bring them home, My precious servers of the light, is to pull them up from the other side.*** You must stand so firmly in the truth of where you are meant to be that you are absolutely unshakable. Unmovable. You must be unable to be fooled ever again by the wily subtle ways of ego and the powerful persuasion of the lie.

You know that I ever point you to the light, to the glorious ever-moving luminescent Love that is My All ever moving forth, so that you may align your heart. Yet for one moment I must show to you what you are not, so that you can have a sense of what you are.

You are not the servants of the lie, the shadow world, the illusion. To put it another way, it is your desire to be able to say, as Jesus did, "The prince of this world hath nothing in me." Now let me show you the subtlety between the two. Oh, yes, I have given you these things before. But I must give them to you again. Too many are being lost to the lie while assuming they are serving Love.

What does it mean, the illusion, the lie, the prince of this world? Beloved ones, it is a mirror image of the truth, but the goal is separation. It is anti-Love or anti-Christ, and on every level it exists in exact proportion to the light, until you cross over from this world. Let Me give you another explanation. In this world, at this level of vibration, there is a veil, a fog, a barrier around the Earth. It is there for many reasons, the greatest of which is ego, for ego is a separate world. It is the living out of the ongoing decision to believe in good *AND* evil, for this is what this entire reality is.

You believe that the Garden of Eden was an historical event that happened way in the past. Yet you have also come to the greater truth that Time does not really exist. So the truth, My beloved ones, is that on one side of the veil is the Eternal Now, the ongoing moment of Creation, the glorious union of the two parts of Myself, the Divine Masculine and the Divine Feminine. And here, in Me, the All in All, I am Love bursting into outward expression! Only Love — Love desiring to give Love, receiving that desire, and the holy union of the two who, of course, together, are the All of Me. Oh, from this union there is the continual creation of magnificence as living, moving, breathing Love.

Within this All, the Love I Am, there rests a special piece of Me, tenderly surrounded by a protective membrane. You are a separated part of Me. You are part of My very heart that has chosen and chooses and is ever choosing to believe there is evil within My being, to believe that you are somehow separate from Me. Oh, sweet humanity, yes, it has grown you. Yes, it has brought you individuality. And in all of this I have carefully kept you, nourished you, loved you, and guided your way. But now is the time to change this choice. This is the leap from the Old to the New.

Yet here in this creation you have made for

yourselves, beloved ones, you have created evil. You, of course, are co-creators. ***What you believe will come to pass.*** So now you are here in a morass of illusion. Yet on the level you are in, it is very real.

There is no way that from within this illusion you can make the decision to be free. You must extract yourselves from this consensual reality where everything is based on dichotomy. You can move closer, and this you must do, for of course your Will is everything. But the final leap, I must do for you. I must do it for you as you give your Will to Me.

Beloved ones, as some of you are seeing, as long as you believe in this reality, you will not be able to shift. The shift is to reverse the polarity, the entire premise by which you live. It is to forever change the background and foreground of the world in which you live. ***It is to realize, beloved ones, that this entire reality is separated from the truth.*** I Am Love. This you already know. You say it to yourselves. You write it in your books. Yet you also believe there exists that which is not Love. Dear ones, this is impossible. Love is All That Is.

The other piece, beloved ones, oh, this one I ask you to take into your being, to hold in your heart, to ponder and pray about — ***you create that in which you believe.***

Of course, this is obvious to many of you – but not quite obvious in every way. If you place your belief on anything but Love, you are creating a separate reality, separate from the One that is All I Am. You are creating a reality that is separate from the rest of All That Is, which is everything, for All I Am is Love and I Am the All of everything.

Oh, precious ones, here is the truth. ***What you and I have called the ego is simply this belief that you are anything else but Love.*** It is the belief that you can live anything else but good. Now, for eons of what you consider as Time, this decision was fine. Yet now, beloved ones, it is time to return. Before "The Garden," we did agree that no matter what happened as you claimed your autonomy as the co-creators you are as My children, a time would come to bring back to Me all the wisdom you had gathered. A time would come when the call of Love would trumpet forth from the voices of the angels, when the very electrons of light would seek recognition in order to deliver their cargo of light. Here we are, beloved ones, children of My Heart.

The call goes forth. Your hearts respond. Yet far too many still remain entangled. So I come to claim you, precious ones. Oh, can you feel this Love pouring into you? Like molten gold I fill you with the living light of moving Love. I call every particle to recognition of My Love, recognition of My Will and recognition, dear ones, of this precious key that only by giving your Will into Mine can you possibly make it across the divide.

Today in this message I blanket the world with this truth, with the bridge to your true reality. Any attention on this world of illusion, this creation of

this false reality, any belief in it keeps it alive, for you are the instrument of its creation.

Oh, beloved ones, what would it mean for you to say, "The prince of this world hath nothing in me?" It would mean you would never again believe the illusion. Yet you do not yet fully know what the illusion is. It would mean knowing the perfection of a world of only Love and not ever, for a moment, believing anything else. It would mean knowing, beloved, without a shred of doubt, that I am your opulence, your glorious supply. It would mean knowing this so well that you would never have a slip and believe that you should learn to precipitate. That is the subtlety of the illusion and your belief in it.

Certainly the majority of you believe that, like Jesus, you will be able to bring forth anything that you need. But you see, here is the difference: Jesus did not decide. I did. Jesus stood in Christ consciousness, which is standing as My Love and only that. It was I, as Love alive in him, I as Love overflowing from his heart, who came forth to fill the need of those who were before him. Jesus had no consciousness of lack. If he had even once had the thought, "Oh, look at these needy, hungry people," dear ones, he would have chosen the "prince of this world." And even if bread manifested, with it would have come the continuation of their lack. None would ever have understood, dear ones, and all I sought to bring through him would have ended up confusion – for it would have ultimately supported the dichotomy. And in doing so, it would have been Jesus doing the work. And well he could have. And the "prince of this world" would have been manifested that day.

Beloved ones, it is too subtle – too subtle for your current consciousness. The mirror image of the illusion means that it looks very similar but the end result is different. The end result is separation. It is putting the power of your co-creative belief at the service of the illusion, the creation of separation, of good **and** evil, of fullness **and** lack, of ego **and** heart. Of your Will **and** Mine.

Place your life in Me, your Will in Mine, oh, precious ones. This is the only way. It is the only way that we can make it across the divide. Otherwise you are continually vulnerable to making the other decision in the moment after this one. Unless you are of Me, then you are of the illusion.

Oh, you could take yourselves up the mountain, higher and higher, into the rarified air of the truth, into the presence of the dawn of truth. But one glance back and we could lose everything. One decision, one still-hidden belief in good **and** evil, and you would be back in the Garden making forever the decision that some were good and some were not. This cannot be true. If I Am Love – and I promise you, I Am - I Am Love and only Love. And I ask you now to let Me show you. Let Me have your Will.

Let Me dissolve you from your separation into your inclusion as My larger heart. Let Me move you beyond that membrane behind which the belief in shadow lives. Oh, beloved ones, I call to you. I tell you that blessed are those who hear and know and give their Will to Me. And oh, the rejoicing when one of you understands. The rejoicing even more if, when in this understanding, you are secured for Love for eternity – for the Eternal Now is all there is. Then, oh, the rejoicing when I carry you across the chasm between the worlds, and you are forever free in Love.

It is urgent, beloved ones. Urgent that you give your hearts, your Will, your lives to Me. And those who have, I send you back to lift the others Home. You have heard that it is your turn, that you are the new Ascended Ones. Your egos cannot take you there, nor can your mind, your intellect, or even your highest consciousness. As long as one iota of the old remains, then the "prince of this world" does have something in you. You cannot do this of yourselves.

I have told you repeatedly of this place to which I call you — the healing of this world, the erasure of inequity, the reigning of peace, and I have continually said, "You cannot get there from here." So do not be deceived, beloved ones. I cannot lose you. I need your hearts to bless and heal and lift the world to freedom. There is no route from here to there. There is no way out through your own volition. There is only the leap that can carry you, and that leap is giving your Will to Me.

Every time you face a choice - what to believe, what to support - I ask you to stop and allow Me to lift you until you can see with My sight. Whenever you find another before you who is reaching to you for assistance, oh, arms raised to you like a little child, STOP. Give your Will to Me. The moment you believe their plight, you lock both of you into it, and no matter how many ways you try, they will never rise above it. Why? Because that "prince of this world" is the illusion of our separateness. *So the moment you even see one as less than perfect you loan your glorious creative power to those who ever promote the darkness.* You give your power to those who continually seek to convince you, My LightWorkers, to lend your glory to their cause. And over and over you do so. Over and over you do so.

Of yourselves, you cannot make this shift. Only in Me can you do it. Only when you become Only Love. And only I can bring you to this. To continue in our current expression, the serpent in the Garden is still offering the taste of the fruit of dual consciousness, the knowledge of good and evil. As long as you continue to eat the fruit, oh, beloved ones, just so long will you be divided, living in the wilderness, believing in lack and tribulation.

Give your Will to Me – decision by decision, and when the sum of your decisions is for only good, the sum of your decision is for My Will not yours, so will be your world. When you are fully in My Will, beloveds, you will be free. All that is of the illusion will simply fall away from you. There is no such thing as karma – not when you are across the divide. How could there be? Karma assumes there is less than good. There isn't. So when you have fully given your Will into Mine, I will show you the truth of Love. You will experience the ecstatic NOW, forever and ever, in this eternal moment. You will be overflowing as My abundance. Not with it, but AS it, for we are ever One. Oh, you will be singing forth in ecstasy, in union with your beautiful SoulMate. You will be that cell of My living heart and the truth will be forever in you.

Then I will give you back your Will, that together we are co-creators. Then, beloved hearts, you will turn and bring the others with you. Then you will see them as they really are, which you will then anchor in them. Holding forth this truth of Love that nothing else exists, you will lift them from the shadow. You will hand their Wills to Mine, for they will see Me in you and see the knowledge of their perfection.

Oh, this is why I train each of you – that this lie of shadows will not confuse you. This is why I ask you to fill your minds with singing gratitude and your SoulMate union with ecstasy. I ask this so that wherever you look you see only Love – even in those who are choosing the lie. Only in Me can you do this. Always from this world will there be judgment, for judgment, beloved ones, is based in the illusion. Judgment is the pervasiveness of that "prince of this world" – for it always compares good and evil.

Oh, yes, it may seem to be otherwise. It may seem to be discernment. It may seem to be helping. Oh, dear ones, it is so subtle. But in truth dear ones, with every such discernment, if you see anything that is less than Love, that "prince" hath something in you.

Of course, I see the enormity of coming out of

this. And this is why I tell you that you can't get there from here. Oh, precious ones, you really can't. Please don't try to prove Me wrong, for so many precious ones are lost. How glad I am that you have made it to this point because it is so subtle. Oh, beloved ones, be very careful, oh, very careful not to fall into judgment. Yes, there is judgment left in you, or you would be completely free. There are bits and pieces that still entice you. But your dedication, your strength of choice, assures your success.

Send forth this message, all who read this, with greatest urgency. You into whose hands this comes are those who will show the way. It is you who are to lift the others up. Remember this, your promise? The time is short (the next ten years) so you must take the leap. You are to be the Ascended Ones who bathe humanity in the truth. But more than this is happening now. It is the Homecoming of all of you. Soon you will see there is no separation, even between you and all that you see, even between you and your beloved precious Earth. You will see that every rock and every tree is a living breathing part of you, and that it lives within your consciousness. You will see that as you are lifted so is it. As you are Home, it all comes with you. So all that you must do, dear ones, is understand your truth in Me. As Me. As Love, the blended One, that is ever two, and ever reflected as you.

In these lines you will find every truth — that while you are learning, you must learn in Me, so that you are safe from the illusion. Then once you know that I Am you, that you are Me, that we are One in living

186

Love, then I will give you back your Will that you will be co-creators. Then our Wills will be blended, beloved ones. Then our Wills are blended. And you will stand as Jesus did, in complete obedience to the truth of Love, that you can add Love to it. Then that Love as you, adds to the Love as Me, and thus are we expanded in you and Love is more than it ever was. My heart will then be grown in you.

Can you feel the honor of this Love? The power of this knowledge? *May your consciousness be the humility of knowing that you must give your Will to Me, that the grace of truth can bring you back into the truth of our perfection.* Raise your precious hearts into Mine, and we are on our way.

*In the singing gratitude
of your hearts,
in union with your SoulMate,
and the clear golden consciousness
waiting for Me,
I can continually plant
the vision of perfection.
You will bring it forth.
At every single moment
I will be using you to
hold in place the perfect world,
for I will be able to feed it through
for you to create,
moment by moment.*

Experiencing Ourselves as in God. Remembrance of Being God's Heart

I am bringing you remembrance of your glorious Love for Me — remembrance of the communion of Love, of living, moving light that is your life in Me. I am bringing you back into ecstasy, which is the true nature of reality. Oh, sweet and glorious children of My heart, I am carefully removing the veil of forgetting that has occupied your minds.

I am not only taking your beautiful hands. I am igniting your magnificent hearts, that once ablaze with Love, you will be the kindling for the fires of Love. I am removing you from your belief in the world, that very soon you will live in Me with such abandon, with such joy, that you will barely be able to see the lie. Only from here in this exploding light, only as your real selves, shining stars in the heavens of My being – only thus will you serve the truth.

Only from the shores of reality can you be of real assistance. Only, My beloved ones, if I Am All There Is to you, will you be able to love the others free. When your hearts are lifted to Me, and both mind and spirit are melted before the fire of Love in your heart, then and only then will I bring to you My precious children.

You must look at them without seeing the lie.

You must look right through it into the truth. You understand this – but not quite enough. It is only from the shores of the New that you can pull them from the freezing waters in which they all are foundering. Only when nothing of the lie is in you will you have the sweet and simple power of the grand divine Love that will set them free. Only when you can look right at them as they wave their fancy flags of ego and not for a moment be distracted by it – then we will move forth.

What it will take, precious ones, is for you to now remember — to remember your Love for Me — not the Love in this current life but the Love that is alive in your spirit. Remember the Love that has brought you, each one, so close, oh, so close to Me. So close that nothing else mattered. So close that you were melted in the heat of your own Love — melted into Me as the Christ is melted, and transformed, rises like the incense of the heavens into the All That I Am.

Can you feel this memory? It is more than believing, more than a vision. It is more than the giving of Love to others. It is the complete knowledge that I Am All, All That Is. All that matters. I Am All in All. All of you. Yes, words are, as always, inadequate. But you know.

You know how you, united as SoulMates, are the song of Love singing within Me. You know the ecstasy of living as My heart – knowing that forever there will be more. You know that in eon after eon (though Time is not counted), you will continually be expanding into this Love that we are. It is the knowing that the ecstasy of your union together as SoulMates, two halves of one cell, is lifted up in the passion of My Love flowing forth forever. It is knowing that you will be washed and washed and washed forever in the flowing cleansing river of light, and that with every washing, you will find Love being revealed to you more clearly.

Can you allow this to touch you now? The knowledge of being My living heart? Of knowing that you are forever within Me? Even now as you are alive in this world?

You are forever within Me. Let this now be the pinnacle of all of your visions and all of your thoughts, because only thus can you possibly begin to grasp what I call you to be. Only when you realize the power of being within Me will you understand how to be grateful, how to pray, even how to love your precious SoulMate. Only then will you realize just how possible, how perfect and how infinite we are together, as you rest in My heart.

Only with this understanding can you truly rest in Me, knowing that there is only infinite Love anywhere around you — knowing, beloved ones, that anything else you see simply can't be real if it is not the infinite Love that I Am.

Only from this vantage point will you understand the New World, or be able to reach back from it to lift the others. Allow yourselves to recall the experience of our Love, of resting within My heart and knowing that everywhere you look there is only Love forever. Oh, but not only some passive state. No. A magnificence of Love that you and your beloved SoulMate grow into forever.

Now carry this knowledge back here – to a world of Love within a world of illusion. Now, in this moment, you can experience this knowing that I Am your reality and you are in My heart forever. So you can see that the assurance of who you are, of what I Am (although you will ever be growing in your understanding), becomes a magnet right here, in this moment, to create this Love around you.

Your place in Me will magnetize the New World to you. It will magnetize the good, the beauty, and a glorious communion in which all life will recognize the truth you at last remember – that you are only Me. Only of Me, only in Me, and the magnificence expands unto forever. Thus will you no longer be confused by the illusion of temporality. You will no longer be trying to "fit in" all the things that I have placed before you — to pray and play, to sing in gratitude, to send Love to all each moment. When you are at last awake in Me, when you are filled with this remembrance, then all the rest will pour forth from you as a multi-colored fountain with every facet interwoven with every other. You will not need to think of anything, because it will simply be a by-product of the central experience of our eternal ecstatic communion.

Then you will really see your beloved SoulMate, for you will see with the true eyes of your remembered spirit. Then you will experience the refreshment of My river of light, for you will be open to its ministrations, that with every washing the truth is more clearly yours. Then, dear ones, then we will turn together to look upon humanity — to wash away the belief in darkness and all the struggling. And you will barely see it, for you will be so anchored in the truth of our Love that what you'll see is the light within them. It will be burning well or only smoldering, but in every case you will do nothing else but fan the flames of their own living heart. I will show you how to do it.

You are very close, beloved ones — a little shift and we are there. A little shift into this sweet remembrance of our Love and communion, yes, and of the world that you inhabit. It should be obvious that you must be fully present, you who reach forth for Me. You must be fully present in this truth until this is all you see – that the world is not solid, not one little bit, and that your heart is in constant communion with absolutely everything you see. If you are fully present in this remembrance of truth, then you will magnetize it to you. The stronger your footing in the truth of our Love, in remembrance of this truth I Am, and its place before you as your SoulMate, the more irresistible this will become to all who are coming toward you. *Do not believe in any of the old world attitudes, beloved ones.* Especially do not believe that there are only a few who can get this and many who will not.

So just as Jesus did, I ask now of you that you go forth to the multitudes. Step right into the illusion and see only the truth. That is the purpose of this preparation. It is for you as it was for him — that *by seeing the perfection in absolutely all before you, you will magnetize it into expression.* This truth is unfailing, even if you do not see it. Thus when you see the truth of Love in my beloved children, even as they live in the shadows of this illusion, the truth will break through the inky darkness within them as surely as sunrise brings the dawn. No matter how long it takes. No matter how it seems.

It is your time, beloveds, those whose heart jumps in joy at the light within these paragraphs. It is your time to go forth, to magnetize the truth of Love right into the midst of the shadows by the power of your steadfast gaze upon the truth. Oh, more than this. By the power of your deep assurance, your inner knowing of our Love and its joyous truth, will you bring it forth around you right into the midst of the Old World. Right into the midst of the illusion will it appear. And all who can see will be blessed profoundly, blessed immediately. Blessed beyond measure. But even if they can't see, your truth must never waver. You, beloved ones, are the good news now going forth. So you certainly don't want to mix up the message by believing in the illusion in any way.

Of yourselves, remember, you cannot do it. But with Me, you can. And you will. Giving your Will to Me is not a passive thing. It is a decision to return to the bathing in the river, a decision to return to the remembrance of our Love so that never ever again are you ever on the outside looking in. You are ever and only completely in Me.

Can you see the difference? This is the shift. No longer are you this little self, looking up with prayers to succeed in loving enough, in living purely, in achieving the ecstasy and in experiencing the SoulMate union. *Rather, you are ever in Me. There is no looking in. There is no looking up. It is from within My heart looking out* that you experience the eternity of joyous learning and expansion of your beautiful understanding of Love. It is from within Me, within the great ever-expanding Love that I Am that My Will can be done in you. Please pray for this remembrance. You must be this larger consciousness of Love. You must be alive in this glory that is My heart, knowing that only I can ever be enough, only I can fill your being. Even the shift to living in the New World must come from within the experience of yourselves as in Me.

The foreground is Me. The All I Am, the glorious amazing living Love is All, and within that Love there is you — My heart. Smaller, as is your heart within your body. But potent. The driving force of the outflow of Love. Thus now when you awake to this concept you will understand the truth of it. From within Me you are alive as My very heart, and that which comes through you comes from all the layers of Love that I Am, in which you ever rest.

All is Me. When you look around, this is all you see. All is fluid. All is moving Love giving forth its light as it vibrates with ecstasy, with flowing joy. Standing in this knowledge you will each reveal the truth of all before you, for living Love illuminates it. So just as the sun evaporates the morning fog, so will the light of My

Will in you, through you, reveal My presence in everything, for in absolutely everything here, there is a truth behind the illusion. Recognized or not, it is there. Alive in Me, you are that sun.

Beloved ones, this is why you must not falter, and why I am growing you so fast. It is your joyful work to promote the vision, to see nothing less and thus never to compromise. If you rest in Me, it will be easy — if you know you are My heart and it is I who love through you. Just as your own heart is not alive until you will it, until you choose to allow Love to pour through – just so it is for Me. All you must be is open that I may love through you. How you stay open is the resting within Me, knowing that of yourself you cannot do it. Yet you must be unwavering in your awareness that you are within Me; that All That I Am is within Me; that nothing is separate, ever.

Within Me, Love is fluid, molten fire, moving forth as creation. This substance of Love, as long as it is molten, is flexible, beautifully dancing forth continually. The substance of Love is never rigid — not in the sunlight of Love's truth as a living moving thing. It is only the closure of human heart and consciousness, away from the heat of the passion that is My Love that allows this rigidity of form and experience.

Thus will you allow this passion, this light and movement, to be how I love through you, My precious heart, the cells of which are the SoulMates of humankind. The moment that you blaze forth together, firmly aware of your presence as My heart, then I may love with you as you love, with the structure of your very own heart. As you stand firmly in this, consciously in the experience of the living light, all those before you will also melt into My presence. They will find themselves standing forth free from the frozen illusory world, flexible in Love again.

You can't do this if you have any belief or any experience of separation from anything. Dear ones, the only possible way that you can accomplish this, now or ever, is to have no separation from Me. No thought of looking up or in. No thought of praying *to* Me. Instead, *your prayers must rise from your consciousness as the acknowledgment of our unity.* They float from you as the sweet rejoicing of your knowing that there is ever more and your willingness to be that. It is the knowing that there is only Love. It is the knowing that as I wash you in this living water, you will ever see more clearly what it means to live in unity, until you have such communion of Love that, truly, you will experience every living thing as US. You will love it as the heart of Me. As you do this while living here, the illusion will melt before you. Ticks will become butterflies as you hold naught but Love within you. Then even butterflies won't be enough – you will want Me to show you more. More of Me. More of Love. And I will then unfold you.

But this is for another time. We are getting ahead of ourselves. For right now, expand your consciousness, increment by increment. Look upon the world again from within My heart. You will see only Love. You will then, just like those to come, allow the experience I provide to filter down into your consciousness, until everything re-zips itself, beloved ones, and unity will stand revealed. There is only ONE, in which all else expresses Love's perfect glory. Love as trillions and Love as one. Nothing else. Love lifting Love, Love gracing Love. Love always and forever expanding. You are the heart of all this. Say, "Yes," to Love! Say, "Yes."

One last comment, beloveds. The moment you are in Love, all else is gone, for it never really was anyway. So you do not need to clean up the past, or undo false thinking. Once you are in the New, in the truth, dear ones, that is all there is. Only if you return to the illusion can the fruits of the illusory thinking touch you. If you are living in light, how could anything not of the light exist there?

So please be done with that cycle of fear – of fearing the fear of your old consciousness. Just let it go and return to Love and then, as I have said, that "prince of this world" will have nothing in you, nothing with which to manifest any thought of disunity. So every time you want to use the Violet Flame or to otherwise erase the result of old thinking, you remain in separation, continuing on with it. Beloveds, in Me there is no darkness. Only Love. Simply come back to the truth rather than wallowing around undoing the darkness.

There is only unity – or there is not. There is nothing in between. You really don't get here in steps, although it seems that way. You simply keep growing in your understanding until finally you get it, and then everything else falls away. Then there is only Me, and you in Me. Only only only Love. What a separation nightmare it would be if you truly had to nullify every wrong, as was the old belief. If you had billions of trespasses to somehow set right and trillions of thoughts of the belief in darkness. Oh, even the best of this is still only a trap, keeping your focus on the world of ego.

Now this does not mean that St. Germain is not real or a great benefactor. It means that the Violet Flame is to help clear the illusion from your precious consciousness – until you can shift. Then the work is done. It is not for looking backwards on millions of wrongdoings, for what are you doing then but believing in them, and believing that so much must be done before you can finally be free of all the negativity you have ever created. What an untrue thought. What a tricky snake the ego is!

No, dear ones, freedom is a happening — a NOW in which you recognize the truth. The progression is only in your consciousness until it can make the shift. Do not look backwards for anything, no matter how enticing! Not even in the name of "saving" My human children. It is a lie. A trap. A trick. Only Love can heal it. Only Love can free it. And Love is ever NOW. Here. Flowing ever perfectly between us – My being and My heart.

We will keep exploring the power of this tricky illusion, for as always you who are reading this, blaze the trail for others. So do not worry if these things rise up – most likely they are now a teaching tool. Simply return to unity, to the solid unified consciousness that there is only Love.

I ask you to do everything solely to hold forth this vision of the truth of Love. You will soon see only Love and nothing else. Then holding forth My Love through you as you dissolve into My Will, I shall hold up mirror after mirror in which I show in truth the perfect self.

I am not just "with you," beloved ones. You have your being in Me. Soon you will understand the power of this.

Love Me
until only I Am real
and you will have all of your answers.
It is the answer in every way
to every question,
forever.
As you grow
in this glorious expansion of yourself,
there will always be another level,
another question,
another adventure,
another discovery of the endless joy
of our being,
expanding in exploding ecstasy
until eternity.

If God Is Love and This World Is Not, Then Obviously This World Is Not Real. Making the Choice

You now understand what it means to be My heart. You are alive in Me. You are My center. You are the place where My Love goes forth! You have also understood the shift — that each of you must go from believing that you are outside of Me in any way — from believing that anything real could be outside of Me — to the understanding that I Am everything.

I Am this world. Humanity is My heart. What does this mean? Oh, beloved ones, for all of you, the answer to this question is the most important answer in your life. Even your temporal minds can understand it. All of you know, at least on an intuitive level, even if you can't quite understand with your minds, that I Am Love. I Am Good.

The reason, beloved ones, that you have been confused is exactly this. Knowing that I Am Love, you have looked at the world and it has thrown you into confusion. So theory after theory has gone forth of how I can be all Love and yet still allow (and by extrapolation, sanction) all this negativity and pain. Here then is the answer. I do not. I cannot, for I Am Love. And finally, oh, finally, you are reaching readiness for the true understanding. If I Am Love, which I Am, and much that you see here is not – then (at last!) obviously, all that is not Love, is not real!

Oh, beloved ones, My beautiful children, so long have I held you in the most tender Love while you were wracked with nightmare after nightmare. How long have all the universes watched as the Tree of Life stood barren in the Garden of this Earth. Now, at last, you begin to wake.

Thus I give you tender support as I begin at last to clear your way. I hold you wrapped in My Love and paint the truth upon the canvas of your consciousness.

"Only Love is real," I now whisper every moment of every day. And to any of you who even barely turn when you hear this sweet inner message of Love, I blatantly light your way. Oh, if you could see it you would chuckle. I now amplify and amplify even the slightest moment of recognition. So those who are opening, in each moment, in every direction you turn, there are waving signs of unity. There are bright lights signaling you, just like a mirror in the sun, flashing forth in Morse code, "Love is All! Only Love is Real!" "Oh, see the Love right here!" In every flower now, there is luminescence. In every encounter, there are messages of truth. In your very earthly dreams, beloved ones, there are streamers of light pouring into the web of subconscious beliefs that create your current world.

Any moment that you listen, all the angels rush toward you, lifting you, lifting you, into proximity to the truth of your own heart.

And even beyond this, I now pour forth the message with potent force and rushing clarity. I deliver to you the truth of Love alive in your life as your SoulMate. Yet even here many of you still find your vision blocked. You find mountains of ego obscuring the Love, and you call to Me for help.

So I come to all of you in every moment, in every way, to say to you that you must now see your choice. You must turn away from the lie. Beloved ones, this means many things to each of you, but most importantly it means the letting go of all you believe this false world can give you. It takes a communion with your deepest self. It takes the power of your Will. Yet I can promise you that if you reach for the world of Love, it will be easy. You will finally see that this illusion is an empty shell and that nothing it offers you will ever satisfy you. It is all a sham, My precious ones, for wrapped within its seeming gifts is the price of your spiritual truth. It is, to put it in familiar terms, the equal to "selling your soul." But what this phrase implies in the current world is always giving up your spirit for some great worldly gain. Oh, My beautiful ones, it is far more subtle. It is the entire web of little lies, those siren songs of the ego. You cannot pick and choose, dear ones. You cannot believe in some and reject the rest of these enticements of the false world.

As you come to Me, as your heart remembers, as you allow yourselves to recognize the longing that has always been within it, there will come a time when you will understand that all of it must go. You will know that you must come to Me and give over your

Will, that you must ask that I bathe you in the river of light that is the living Love around you. This river is the dividing line between the false world and the real. You have sensed it. Other cultures have named it. Yet the subtle negativity then claimed it before you could bathe yourselves in the living truth. It became something experienced after death. Thus was it, too, removed from you.

Now, as with so many things, I give its truth back to you. To be washed in this living and moving Love is to be lifted and released from the dream. And what is this washing, beloved ones? It is the washing away of illusion. It is the sweet cleansing of all the untruth of the subtleties of separation. It is also a question to your consciousness. Are you willing to let go of the "things of this world"?

Oh, there are many ways to explain this to you. But the most accurate is this. As long as your consciousness believes the illusion, there will never be room for the truth. You must will this cleansing. You must choose the experience. Whether by small incremental steps as you slowly regain your awareness of Love, or by the great splash of giving yourself at once and completely over to Me.

In this cleansing you will experience the releasing of illusion. For some it will be as nothing; for others it will be a rending. If you are deeply woven into the illusory world and the belief it can ever satisfy, this experience can be very difficult. Yet your hearts will push you to it.

All the ways your ego has convinced you that it can offer you satisfaction, telling you that it is worth going after the things of this world — all those you must release.

For many of you, you will wade across the river of living Love, taking your time and making it gentle. This is fine, beloved ones, as long as you continue to move toward Me. If you do it this way, then (seemingly) over time you will be shown all of the ways the illusion entices you. Do you dream of having wealth? Do you (secretly) want admiration? Do you want others to need you, so you continue to see them as someone who has problems? And, oh, most importantly, My beautiful children, do you see any other person as less than perfect?

Do you believe in the false presentation of reality in any way? If you do, this light will cleanse you. Yet you must be willing for it to succeed. You must choose, and choose, and choose to see only the truth, which is the world of Love.

Then, precious ones, I will gently lift you as the time arrives when you refuse the dream any longer. When it only makes sense to you that this must be illusion, for only Love is our reality! When you know without ever doubting that Love is all you want, all you need, that your only desire is to bring to your brothers and sisters this truth — when you completely give your little Will away to Me, then, oh, in sweet surrender will you take up your residence in your Home of Love, which is the only truth. And you will know without ever a waver that you rest in Love in My heart, as My heart, beloved ones, for you are the very cells themselves. And, oh, so deeply and completely surrounded by My eternally expanding support of Love, the illusion will be gone from you completely. Here. Now. In this world. Not after dying, or even ascending, but simply as your truth finally recognized.

This is where we are now, My beautiful diamonds, those of you who are shining forth the prisms of your true selves, your multi-dimensional, multi-layered passionate and glorious beings. You are now recognizing the dream (or rather, the nightmare), finally! And now choice by choice or in one great movement, you are renouncing the illusory world.

Oh, I will wrap you forever in the glorious shimmering expansion of My Love as it flows and dances forth from you on every side. And, oh, once you have been washed clean of the illusion (that I could ever be anything other than good) and recognized yourselves, you will at last be truly functioning as My heart. Hidden in Me – just as your physical heart is hidden in you – untouched by the false in any way, I will pour and pour and pour through you My Love to all My other children, precious diamonds also, yet still hidden.

Now to bring it into you I ask you to embrace the awareness of yourselves as My living heart. Here, of course, you are ever with your SoulMate. And here of course, you relate only to the real.

Come close to Me. Oh, closer, closer. Feel My Love revealing you as the center of My very being, as the heart of Love through which I love. Beloved ones, this is what I ask of you now, the acceptance of this as your only truth. The more you accept it, the more refreshing the bath, as the river of loving, dancing glorious Love washes the illusion away. The more you accept, the more you open to feel the passion of My Love flowing outward through you, the more true your experience when you interact with this world, for there will be no illusion before you.

We have used the words, "Give your Will to Me," to begin this process of remembrance — remembrance of your truth and the truth of this world and of course, of My beloved humanity. Of course, you are never separate from anything. That is only the dream, or illusion. So may the giving of your Will be the first part of your shift into the continual experience of your truth as My heart.

There is no way to describe for you this experience, beloveds. No way but in choosing it that you can ever understand what it means to be the heart of God. Let yourselves imagine it! Oh, imagine and imagine and imagine what it means to be the vessel of eternal Love pouring perfectly forever. And as you imagine, your memory will start. As you choose to love the truth, you'll begin to feel My Love pour through you – oh, nothing can prepare you.

This little world, this little self that you believe you currently are, is covering a truth so big it is the heart of Love of All That Is! Take that into your imagining. Soon you will become that great and glorious river your very selves. Soon together, in unity as SoulMates, the Love poured through you, beloved ones, can span and move and illuminate the entirety of everything. So to illumine this sweet Earth and to free the other precious ones will be only a moment of your attention.

I am reaching for you. Come, make the switch. Release this world and anything that possibly can hold your precious attention, for I promise you (it's obvious) that the equivalent of whatever it is, in the real world will be magnificent compared to this puny imitation — an imitation carefully manipulated to drain the power and to freeze the Love. So though it might seem difficult to let it go, whatever it is, the reward, dear ones, is glorious and endless and eternal.

Remember. If I Am only and ever Love, then only Love is real. Yet in this lie you will never know a taste of who we are. So you must see the illusion in order to choose, to look at the darkness and refuse it entrance, and you are on your way. Choose every moment. See only Love, and turn to remember you are in Me. You are My heart, eternally.

Jesus had no boundaries.
He did not see himself
as a human being,
even when expressing thus.
He saw himself only and ever
as a vessel of My Love.
This Love became
his complete and total identity.

Love Me Until Only I Am Real
and You Will Have All Your Answers

Love Me until only I am real and you will have all of your answers. It is the answer in every way, to every question, forever. As you grow in this glorious expansion of yourself, there will always be another level, another question, another adventure, another discovery of the endless joy of our being, expanding in exploding ecstasy unto eternity.

Oh, beloved ones, you are growing in your consciousness in two arenas. You are expanding your understanding of how it is to be My heart, to know that you are ever held within Me, surrounded by the unending Love that is My being. You are also learning what it is like to be supported perfectly by Love as it expands around you in every direction, in tenderness in its acknowledgment of you. Yes, you know that as My heart, you must bow in surrender, that I truly may pour My great Love through you – that I may tip you gently to pour out through you My blessings upon humanity. You can understand the truth of your presence, the perfect expression of a cell within My heart with your SoulMate, as the heart of All I Am.

Yet some of you are asking: "Teach me how to be You while being here in this mind and body. If You are All and we are in You, then what of those words that Jesus spoke, continually, that You were in him?"

God immanent and God transcendent — these words express this perfectly. This, dear ones, is part of the shift of which I have so long spoken. The background and the foreground of our life will change as you accept your place as the heart of Me. The answer is exactly this. Love Me until only I Am real.

Now I will tell you how to do this. Yet as in everything, the experience will be a gentle building of blessing upon blessing upon blessing until only I exist in you and until every thought and word and deed is My perfect Love expressing. This personality will become for you only the necessary medium through which I speak and love and serve, to bless My precious children. You will come to know only your truth as Love and as My expression in every moment.

How we do this is simply this answer I have given – taken into every moment of your life. ***Love everything before you as Me.*** Love yourself as Me. Look in the mirror and see only My perfection. How amazing is it that I would love you this much, that I would come here with you? That I would help create these eyes, these lips – to see, to speak – and place here as you, My heart, for Us to love through?

Turning to your precious Love, you see that only I exist in the miracle of Love's expression. Imagine creating hands that I might touch you! Eyes in which you are reflected. Oh, and such a unique expression that I may be your SoulMate! And look! Look at the verdant trees, the Love I am, formed to shade, to bless, and to inspire you, to paint your daily world, with life expressing right before you.

We are All That Is, for we cannot be separate. The moment that you truly know this, that everywhere you look you know that I am there, loving you as what you see, then you will have the miracle. The Love "within" you and the Love "without" will bridge the gap, and the identity as a separate self, the "skin" of this illusion will evaporate. It will evaporate as the morning mist you see upon the lake evaporates in the sun's warmth. It will evaporate. Then you will know yourself as Christ, as only Love in Me. You will see your world as it truly is – as perfect Love in myriad expression – as Us, beloved ones, giving expression to our joy.

In this moment you will no longer have a singular identity – and yet you will deeply know yourself. You will know yourself in our glorious expression of My joy pouring forth as you.

Yes, I know. I know that your challenge always is to take these things into your life and bring this forth as experience. Oh, but you are very close.

You have understood that separation is a dream within your little mind – the part of you that now believes you have an identity other than Me. Let Me address this for you. You are a unique expression of Love. You are a cell alive within My heart, together with your SoulMate, that the All of Love is perfectly reflected in the parts. Yet every part is a singing joy, a note in the great song of My Love. Thus, beloved ones, in this shadow world your current identity is a shadow reflection of your true self. Yes, most things here have a basis in the Real (most things that are good). So you will not lose your identity. You will only find that We are You. You will find that your identity is Me, expressing My Love in you, as you. *As you recognize Me within you, as you see Me loving you as your SoulMate, as you find your heart affirming for you that everything you touch or see is Me sharing this experience, you will get your true identity.*

Do you know how you can feel Love resonating within you in your heart? How it vibrates within you and you can feel the presence of My Love alive in you? This is as you are to Me. I feel you in My heart. I feel you resonating. I feel you, of course, with glorious clarity, while you have just begun to acknowledge this experience. So as I feel My heart, you are there — you, the two who are this cell. You have a vibration, a note, a buzz, an energy that is completely and totally recognizable, always and forever to Me. As I love, I am forever conscious of that sweet exalting vibration that is you. As I love, that unique vibration, that glorious energy, goes forth to touch and bless. I truly do fill Creation with you, for I cannot do otherwise.

Thus, you are everywhere. You are in everything I love. So in truth you are the consciousness of Love that is the power of My moving living Love, expressed through this cell of My heart as the energy you are. When I say "you" in all of this, please be aware that I am always speaking of the two of you, for together you are the vibration, the cell, the opening, and the energy.

All of you, My human children, are not (and never were) children in the current understanding. I have used this word so you could relate to how I love you, but now we must replace this outworn concept. You are not less than I Am in any way. You are My very Love as it pours through My heart.

Beloved ones, it may take a moment (as reckoned by the All of Love) for you to let go of all your recent definitions of who and what you are and to allow yourselves to be the communion of Love that you really are.

This Earth (as I have often told you) is not a separate entity. It is you, as My Love, splashing forth into expression. Right now this is what you are focusing upon – this Earth, this life, this lovingness. As soon as you fully recognize yourself, then you will begin to tune your consciousness to the greater truth – that you, too, are in everything. You are a specific vibration of My Love going forth. Then you can grasp that you can experience any and all of everything there is, simply by recognizing that you must be in it. You must! I forever love with My whole heart (of course). This means that absolutely every single human being is present in absolutely everything.

I have explained to you before that this personality is a tiny speck in the entirety of your being, when I was explaining your presence in and as the entire expression of Earth. Well, that is how I always do this – I give you pieces that I build upon, and your eager interest and heartfelt prayers have brought this subject back again, more quickly than anticipated.

So you are the unique vibration of the Love that you are, alive in absolutely all that I love. This will tell you two very important things. You do not really exist in anything (and I mean anything) that is negative, for negativity is not of Me. It is only (only!) by your agreement that you can even pretend to be a part of anything negative. Secondly, it shall become obvious that your having your attention focused through this little peephole called personality is also not true.

Yes, you went forth to develop an identity that you could become a sovereign consciousness with Me, in the celebration of our living Love, splashed forth together across all of Creation. Yes, you are an expansion of what I Am because you are to hold that vibration that is uniquely you – forever. It does not fade. It does not become lost in a bigger song. Nor does it become secondary to what I create. You, My heart, are the harmony - in millions of glorious parts - as your unique vibrations sing forth with Mine, and all Creation is expanded and enriched in it.

So, beloved ones, can you sense the truth of this message? You must now come to know yourselves as you really are. Oh, the glory of our combined song! Beloved ones, please imagine it. I do not say this idly, nor as a one-time thing. I want you to begin right now to imagine this truth of your Christed beings. Imagine your truth as you accept that you are My Love in perfect expression in you, and that My Love is the song of Creation in which you, dear ones, are the harmony.

To become Christed is simply to know these things and for them to become your reality. All you have to do is go a little further than your current consciousness. All you have to do is reach for Me in passionate Love in any direction, and you will break through this membrane that has you believing you are separated from everything around you. By saying you can go in any direction, I mean that you can recognize yourself in union with Me everywhere you look, EXCEPT into negativity. So you can look at Nature, at the glorious abundance of our expression of fertility, of creative energy and nurturance. You can look upward at your highest vision of Me, and you can recognize our union there. You can use anything in which the true light is held, any path, any saint, any teacher, as long as your goal is to break free of the illusion that there is anything but us, expressing the utter joy of having each other forever.

I love you passionately. I love you exuberantly. Abundantly. Oh, in the most joy-filled rejoicing. Why else would I create you if you were not the most beautiful gift that I could ever give Myself? Oh, why would I even bother, if I Am everything?

Our communion is My fulfillment. We share Creation as I pour you forth, My loving heart (remember everything is motion), and you expand My greatest ideas. As you go forth as My living moving heart, then you add to My song of Creation. You bring in new harmonies. Even you know in your limited perception (your temporarily limited perception) how much adding harmonies enriches and fills out a song. It doesn't even take a musical ear to know it!

Well think, dear ones, how you are millions of harmonies, harmonies coming from harmonies — think of what this does! You enrich with such beauty the living song of life. Of course, you understand that even in this idea of music that you can currently comprehend lies a glorious truth of a real song that you cannot ever hear while in this limited consciousness. Oh, as you accept our great truth, this song will come forth directly, as you. Your heart will know its beauty, and suddenly a sweet refrain will be added to Creation.

I give you what I can to entice you to break free, to go for the recognition of who you are with Me. With Me, dear ones, is the ultimate key. Because step-by-step I have been leading you to the opening of this concept, this understanding.

You can feel who you are. You can feel this experience of our wondrous joy-filled communion. You can first allow it to pour forth unimpeded to your SoulMate. Unimpeded, beloved, is the word here. Allow Love to live you. To live you. To live you. Open to this. Ask Me for it. For this is not a passive process. It is the step above the hollow reed. It is the passionate, exuberant action or (yes!) feeling of throwing yourself into the river. It is the feeling of jumping forth as who you really are and becoming only the identity of living, passionate, giving Love.

Then begin to do this with everything, with everyone. Pour your entire self upon them. Do this to someone standing in front of you (whom obviously I have brought to you). Know that you are to become the river of living Love that rushes forth to them, so that you, in your little identity, disappear in it. And know, too, beloveds, that if there is anything that you see in them that you judge imperfect, that very thing still has a hold on you. If whatever it is can still make it through all this Love to actually show up on the screen of your consciousness, it means that as you pour yourself forth as our passionate Love, you are loving yourself free as well. Ultimately, all you see anywhere will be Me. Only. That is when you will make your leap into Christ consciousness, as we now name it — into the living experience of nothing but this ecstatic and exuberant union of Love. That is when you will pick your direction – what to look at to break through the membrane, and to become only and forever the Love of My heart.

God greeting God. God making Love to God. God marrying God. God feeding God, grooming, petting, God admiring God with wings, as the hands that are trees with the leaves that are the rhythm section as they shiver in the wind. This you will find as your experience, and you'll begin to recognize yourself as the Love within all of these things – all the movements of the symphony. Together, we are the creator of this symphony. We together are the conductor, and we are each and every instrument whose lovely voices express our song. And we become the song itself, flying, dancing, winging forth in every plane, in every world.

You are here to rend the veil, to expose the

membrane, and to remind the others. In seeing them within yourself, we are assured of their opening. While you are each a unique individual, you together with your SoulMate, you are a part, together with all of them, of My one heart. So as the cells gain recognition, just so will the experience penetrate the whole of which you are a part (immanent) and an awakening is imminent.

Imminent. Close. About to happen. That word is perfect, for imminent means "perched on the edge," about to fly forth. It also means "closer than your hands and feet." Imminent. It is imminent that you shall transcend your limited recognition of yourself.

It is time to begin our Love affair, the Love affair with life, recognizing our communion in and as each and every thing you see (that is other than the shadow). As you do this, it will be effortlessly clear that this shadow world is not anything real. Oh, I know, it seems so very real. Many of you are quite enticed by it – especially in the idea of "saving it." But precious ones, here is what you will find. The only way to "save" any of it is to completely turn from the negativity. As you do this, as you exuberantly accept the truth of our Love, I promise you, you will not see negativity. Its existence will fade.

Beloved ones, if there is nothing in you to attract the negative, then all you will see is Me. So one could be standing in front of you who is deeply entangled in the illusion, but you will not lend your Love and your power to it by recognizing any negativity at all.

Instead, dear ones, you will look at them tenderly and you will only see yourself in them, Me in them and Love in them. In so doing, you can set them free. Remember what I have told you, what we named "unconditional positive regard?" Remember that in a perfect world (which is what you will live in) every person would know themselves truly by seeing only Love and admiration in their parents' eyes? Well, beloveds, in that moment you will begin for them that early step in the awakening, the step where you see Me as your loving parent. You, having recognized yourself as Me, will give to others this greatest gift. Believe Me, it will be recognized. They will grasp that you see nothing in them that is anything less than perfection. Their evolution into true Love will have begun.

Then will you most definitely be in the world, not of it, for your world will not be theirs. Your world will be ours. Yet by now you know that the only way to ever bring the New World forth is to see it now, in front of you, lending no power to the illusion of negativity, for in truth it does not exist. It is only a little pocket of separation that caught the fancy of some of My children. Soon it will fade away.

Study these things with an open heart and a joyous seeking spirit. Study yourself in everything good, in everything sweet, and in everything beautiful. Make Love to yourself in the form of your SoulMate, and then notice – there is something in all of these. Something else is looking back at you in all these many mirrors. It is Me, of course; for when you see yourself truly you must acknowledge that I Am there. I Am in you, as you are in Me. Yes. But you are not this little self. You are not limited in any way. So please don't try to listen to Me somewhere inside this smaller self. There is no room for me there.

When Jesus said, "The Father is in me," beloved ones, he recognized himself as all the Love in everything. So do not wait for My "still small voice," for nothing could be farther from the truth. No, recognize that you must be the truth of your expanded self, and then you can say, "God is in Me." Yet even then, you will see a new truth, for rather than Me being in you and you also being in Me, you will recognize there is only one, and we are thus in everything.

These things are beyond your smaller mind, but they are right here in your heart. Love Me until I Am all you see – and you will recognize yourself.

So you,
My beloved way showers,
must walk this path yourselves
until you can traverse the worlds with ease.
You will go forth into the New,
stepping through the doorway,
yet coming back just as easily,
so that you can bring another group
and another
and another —
until enough of the cells of My heart
accept the truth and live it.
Then, as you've been shown in many ways,
the truth will spread exponentially
to every cell of Love within Me.

The Emotion of Divine Love
Is the Only True Power in All of Creation

The emotion of divine Love is the only true power in all of Creation, for the emotion of Love is the glorious joy-filled pouring forth of My being. I pour forth into every reach of every cosmos, be they vast and brilliant or tiny and microscopic. This explosion rushes outward, through All I Am, throughout forever as I Am forever, exploding forth in this glorious moment of Creation. It rushes inward. It rushes to fill and enliven absolutely everything. This movement of My never-ending Love is the one force, the one movement that is life. There is none else.

It is in the power of your being to co-create Love and to push it forth that is your crowning glory. It is the great sign of your truth as My heart that you alone are the generators of this force. With it you also may nourish life.

Yet here you are in a shadow-filled world, alive with the opposite of living Love. And you, My beloved beings of light, My precious cells of My awakening heart – you are remembering. It is stirring in you, this remembrance of the living moving glory of Love. It is lifting your vision as you reach up toward it. There is something whispering within you, something that tells you that this Love is also yours. Something is telling you that in its rushing sparkling movement is your complete supply. If you could simply reach up and fill the cup of your heart and consciousness, it would provide you forever with all your abundance and good.

Yet in this shadowy world of illusion, it can be very confusing, for it truly is like a hall of mirrors. The trick of the illusion is the reverse of truth. Thus you still recognize it. It catches your attention. Yet now, beloved ones, you must quickly come to distinguish the truth of Love from its shadow self.

Yes, there seems to be Love in this world. But just as in a hall of mirrors, if you follow it, it leads you ever onward, bouncing images that never quite fulfill, never do reveal the Love that you seek. So it is for you, My LightWorkers, light seekers, those who are now awakening. The very things that were enough before are not enough now. The very ways that those seeking used to raise themselves, even recently, have now become outdated. These ways have now become a stumbling block as you seek to truly free yourselves. Now, beloved ones, you must make the choice to free yourselves completely from this house of many mirrors that is the current life on Earth. And remember this. Most of you who are the first have come specifically to mark the way for those who follow after you. *So there comes a point where every thought you have and its resolution, every lesson that you learn, every single revelation is in your life only for those who will follow you – that you may lead them forth.*

Now we come to another fork, another place where the path splits, another moment where the choices of eternity must come to play in incarnated life. Every person must make the choice which world they will support. Beloved ones, you are so very close that all you must do is make this shift and you open the doorway into the real, into the truth, and out forever from the refracted light in the hall of mirrors. *That shift, beloved ones, is choosing the one and only power alive in all the universes and claiming it, living it, oh, becoming it in every sense – the truth of living moving Love as living dancing energy.* Oh, it is for you to now become the open pathway for this moving Love, and it will pour in to lift and free the world.

Doing this, for some of you, will take real discernment. Yet with every taste of the real emotion of radiant moving singing Love, you will know. It is this Love moving through your being that will create the transformation. In choosing to feel only this Love, divine Love, true Love — it is in doing this, beloved ones, that the Love "within," rising up in joyous ecstasy, will meet the Love "without," dissolving the membrane of this pocket of Time and becoming a conscious part of All I Am.

Words cannot ever express this Love, yet you must search within for this experience. You must give your all to this, every effort, every prayer, for underlying everything, all you are and ever will be and the creation of absolutely everything, is this living glory of moving Love. *Oh, precious ones, you must make its acquaintance — that Love that is your only reality,* yes, but even more – so that you can feel this Love that is All We Are, that you can experience the glorious miracle. Exploding forth, rushing outward, these currents of Love animate everything.

The emotion of Love – of real Love, divine Love – is the only true power there is. Yes, beloveds, you are to feel this. You are to feel a Love so powerful and so perfect that from it comes All That Is.

Now here is how to do it. This will, of course, be a growing truth, a series of leaps and shifts and jumps until you are the experience of living Love, the feeling I Am and thus that you are. Truly you can catch only a glimmer of this, yet, oh, every glimmer is worth everything. Yes, I am leading you through the doorway, out of this pocket of protected Time – that you may feel the cosmic winds upon your sweet uplifted faces, that you may know yourselves among the stars, for truly, My beloved ones, they are wrapped in you, for they are ever alive in the sea of moving Love.

Be prepared! Be prepared for the moments where you make the shift into the real. Be prepared to take a moment outside of time. Yet for all of you now reading this, I ask you to remember. You are not here to do this for yourself. You are only here to show the way to others.

So this, of course, is your very first decision – to give your Will to Me; for of yourselves you cannot do this. Only I can accomplish this. Only I can pull you through the veil. Only I can lay the pathway through the stars for all humanity to follow, for you, beloveds, have neither the vision nor the full power of living Love.

Secondly – and this is SO important, you *must acknowledge LOVE as All.* All. And more than all. More than you can even dream. Nothing else is true. Now let Me show you why.

The current path of LightWorkers in general is still behind a step, which is why I come to urge this shift. On the current path is held the belief in the power of the Violet Flame. Now I do not dispute this. I want only to show you that now, beloveds, you must move beyond it. *If you choose the Violet Flame, in just that choice and nothing else you acknowledge negativity.* You place your belief firmly in the illusion, and from this comes forth the entire spectrum.

You believe that you need to transform thoughts of negativity, which also lends itself to the belief that if you slip and have negative thoughts, then they are now real and moving toward you. This acknowledges Time. Also inherent in this thinking is the acknowledgment of whole strata of beings who feed on negativity, who will use someone who has slipped – all the way down to upholding the belief in hell, with thousands of souls trapped in their own hatred and terrible negativity. *IS THIS THE WORLD YOU CHOOSE?*

Stay here for a moment.

Dear ones, everything I have spoken of is real within its level — real in this pocket of Time and mis-creation. Oh, yes, it exists – but not in Reality. It only exists here, beloved ones, only here in the drama of your illusion.

You cannot ever escape this "passion play" (of the lower-self variety) if your attention is here, for where your attention is, there your heart is. This I promise you. Thus from the seemingly positive choice for the Violet Flame has come the placement of your precious attention.

Pause again to think upon this, and all its implications.

Now here I must say something very important. There is a place for the Violet Flame. It is a powerful and loving gift for the freeing of humanity. It is invaluable to those who are completely trapped. It is their first wedge against the nightmare, their first choice to recognize the illusion. However, I am speaking here to those of you who understand the meaning of Christ consciousness. I am speaking here to those of you who are the leaders. If you have picked up this book or otherwise found these words in your hands, you are ready. Your heart knows the truth of Love and your spirit hungers for the true emotion. You are ready to rend the veil, to mark the path, and ready to be fed the true manna, that of our living moving Love.

So, dear ones, the other path, the one for you to follow, is the decision to live only Love, now, even here in the midst of this illusion. The decision to see only Love is to trust that in any moment this living, breathing, pulsing and glorious river of living dancing light-filled Love *CAN* and will wash you clean of all of the illusion, in this moment and in the next. Should you buy into the illusion, in the next moment, if you turn back to Me, if you ask to be bathed in the river of Love and light, that in that moment you are free. *The illusion only exists through your belief in it. Thus, there is no karma, no reaping what you sow, no coming toward you of that mistaken thought, no gathering by it of substance or energy. Only if you believe it, can it be so. Nothing but Love exists in truth.*

Yet, as you make this shift within – as you look at everything and see only Love – then you must come back into the illusion, that you may lead the others. I will give you all the truth. I place it in your hands and hearts. I will ask you to digest it, to absorb it, and to practice it as if you were the others, so that you will know the path by heart so you can lead them to the doorway.

You must lead them to that hole that we have now created in the membrane around this hall of mirrors. Oh, you can bring the others there, and standing hand-in-hand with them, beloved ones, you can show them the truth. You can show them the glorious fields of living stars through which runs this beautiful river of living Love. You can show them the angels with their wings of faith, and tune their ears to the celestial chorus. And then you can turn and "give them a push," that they may become those flying SoulMates! Then you go back and get some others.

With every group of precious souls, you will have a path to show them, a path of SoulMate ecstasy.

Of praying without ceasing,
Of praying always gratitude,
Of letting Love become them,
By giving truly.

And, as I've always said in every Holy Scripture,

By loving Me with all your heart,
With all your soul,
With all your mind,
With all your strength.

(And, naturally, then you will always love all others
as yourself!)

You will follow this path until this Love fills all of
your beings and reaches up beyond the veil, joining with
the Love I Am — the Love "within" meeting the Love
"without" and becoming one with that glorious river.

Emotion is your greatest power. It creates the
illusion. As I have told you for some time now,
thoughts must be filled and fired with the energy of
emotion in order to come forth – be this the reversed
emotions of selfishness in all its forms of anti-Life, or if
it is the truth of Love, the divine Love that is Creation.

So I will repeat to you the idea that sums it up.
Because you are My very heart, I have ever and always
brought forth your hearts' desires. Your hearts' desires,
beloved ones, are the feelings you accept as truth. *Thus
do we now refine these feelings to make them only the
belief in Love* — Love that is the most amazing good,

the greatest and most tender grace.

No longer can humanity have the lie within their hearts – the lie that is belief in lack, in negativity, and even in death, for these have been the feelings that have dropped into their hearts to become this current shadow world.

So you, My beloved Way Showers, must walk this path yourselves until you can traverse the worlds with ease, going forth into the New, stepping through the doorway, yet coming back just as easily, so that you can bring another group and another and another – until enough of the cells of My heart accept the truth and live it. Then, as you've been shown in many ways, the truth will spread exponentially to every cell of Love within Me.

The path has split. Now it splits again. Now - with a little cosmic humor – there may be some who call this splitting stuff, a "splitting of hairs." This is only because they do not see the subtlety of this powerful truth – that *what you believe (feel, accept in your heart as real) you create, and that you each must carefully extrapolate the truth behind every decision.* Only thus can you possibly see that something as good (truly) as the Violet Flame can, at a point, become an impediment to the birth of truth within you. So it is with every decision.

So, I have given you the breakthrough experience, where Love "within" meets Love "without." I now take you past gratitude to the consuming prayers of living Love where you give to Me your every breath in the consuming pouring forth of Love to Me. In this I am speaking of the pathway through the veil. It is taking the energy, the purity, the vibration attained through your continual praying gratitude and lifting it into all-consuming Love. This Love is directed, purposefully and powerfully, with all your strength, with all your heart, soul, and being — pushing it, pouring it, moving it as great emotion — to Me. In its power, it rushes up to My Love as it is pouring in to you. In the experience, the two shall meet and rend the veil, and you are one with Me. Yet still you are ever your beautiful self, for you have learned how to move Love. You have learned how to become co-creators – for you have become completely the living moving emotion of divine Love.

It does all perfectly fit together. Love immanent – I Am in you. Love transcendent – I Am All That Is, joined together in co-creation.

It is exquisitely simple and pure. It is always and forever the learning of who you are and of what is real. You were waylaid by a fantasy that something else could be real, and you explored it. It has illuminated you immensely, once you can see its truth. Seeing the truth is all you must do – and all you must show (teach) your precious brothers and sisters.

Yes! The illusion can even be very beautiful – but it obscures the true beauty behind it. So it is with human Love, beloved ones — human in the illusory sense, versus divine Love, which is real in you. In all the sweetness of human Love, it does not point you out of the illusion, for hidden within is your belief in its passing and in all the ways it will cause you pain. ***This is why you must choose only your SoulMate and choose only to love them as you love Me, for this will affirm the truth of your relationship, that it is forever and ever and it is divine in its nature.*** It will also affirm for you together the truth of your being – that you will love Me, directly and in each other – with all your heart, soul, mind, and strength. Doing so, you will always affirm the eternal truth – that Love will always lift you up, will bless you and will free you, and that by placing this kind of Love in your heart then your heart's desire is to be who you really are, divine Love's co-creators.

Love Me until only I am real, and you will know yourselves (SoulMates)...

You will accomplish this by loving Me with all your heart, with all your soul, with all your mind, and with all your strength. This will bring you through the veil to the glorious joining of Love that is you (SoulMates) and Love that is Me, and in this you will...

Love your neighbor (your brothers and sisters of humanity) as yourself, and thus you will bring them with you.

Showing you how these simple truths are recorded in your culture's scriptures shows you how what is true will continue to grow in its meaning, in its revelation. This ever-deeper revelation is how the truth of Love stays a living thing, even flowing forth here in the midst of the illusion. All you must do is recognize it. The river of Love - it is here, even here. Follow it back Home. Show this to the others.

TO THE READER

If you have resonated strongly with what you have just read, please know that there are in process more books of Messages from God that continue the thrilling journey to Christ consciousness. ***Say "Yes" to Love, Giving Birth to the Christ Light*** will be published within the next months.

On the pages that follow are three powerful personal communications to each of us, given through the Messages from God. If you ***Make a Personal Commitment to God,*** we have been assured that you will have a visible, tangible, personal experience of God. ***Dissolving Impediments to Opening the Heart*** came as a meditation. It is given to assist us in releasing any blocks to an open heart and to accelerate reunion with our SoulMate. In response to God's request for the widest possible distribution of ***A Letter from God to Humanity on Creating a World of Love,*** we include it here.

We also invite you to visit our active Circle of Light website, www.circleoflight.net where excerpts and complete Messages from God are posted on many subjects. There is also a page of readers' questions with answers that elaborate upon the content of the Messages. You may also join our monthly email list for a monthly Message from God.

May you live with an open heart in a world of Love every moment.

The Team at Circle of Light

YOU CAN HAVE A PERSONAL RELATIONSHIP WITH GOD

Make A Commitment To God Now.

God is preparing a net of living Love with which to lift the world, and is asking you to be a part. In recent Messages, God said "My Love is pursuing you. My grace now comes to stand before you, harder and harder to ignore—until beloveds, it will take more strength than all the legions of the lie to keep My grace from touching you and awakening you, My heart, into the Love you are."

God asks that you **make a written Commitment to open to God** (by whatever name is comfortable for you) **and begin a daily communion with God for yourself.** We have found that a wonderful time to do this is in the morning before getting out of bed, but it may be done at any time that fits your personal life schedule. The important thing is that it is done at least once daily and with consistency.

God has promised that each person who does this will have direct experience of a personal communion with God, "as long as they keep hope alive and the living spirit connection in their life." It is each person's responsibility to keep the connection open. **"You will have all the light of Heaven coming to you."**

God has also asked that we at Circle of Light Spiritual Center act as a bridge, and each day bless and amplify every Commitment we receive, thus raising its vibration and magnifying the effect of its words. "...there will be those who begin to fly – whose hearts have wings – and they open to Me with great hunger and great joy. These we shall quickly add to the team of those who are part of the LightHouse."

God also has asked that each person make a list of the things for which they are grateful—"to include the success of their connection to Me, and a list of people to whom they wish to send My Love."

In Love, we deliver these instructions from the Messages from God as to how to proceed.

MY COMMITMENT TO GOD
How To Proceed

Please fill out both Parts I and II below, and your name, address and/or email address. This may conveniently be done on index cards. Keep a copy of what you have written for yourself to review several times daily. Mail or email a copy of your Commitment to us so that we may amplify it at Circle of Light Spiritual Center.   If you wish, you may go to our website, www.circleoflight.net to post your Commitment.

Part I

Please do use your own words but we give sample wording to assist you. You are of course not limited to what we suggest below. Be passionate; be real; speak your heart. Write in the present tense, as though what you are doing has been already accomplished. Please KNOW that as you make this Commitment, you WILL begin to have direct experiences of God.

Sample wording: "I am making a deep commitment to open my heart and call God personally into my life each day. I am taking responsibility to maintain this connection, and I ask Circle of Light to amplify it for me in every way possible."

Part II

(a) Please write a list of things for which you are grateful, including the success of the above connection you are making with God. Again use the present tense. (b) Please also list people to whom you wish God to send Love.

MAIL OR EMAIL
a copy of your Commitment to:

Circle of Light Spiritual Center
3969 Mundell Road
Eureka Springs, AR 72631
connect@circleoflight.net
www.circleoflight.net

Dissolving Impediments
To Opening The Heart

The following Meditation on ***Dissolving Impediments to Opening the Heart*** was given through Yaël Powell at Circle of Light on Tuesday November 19, 2002, during a group meeting. Once you have done this Meditation and established this connection with God, there is no need to repeat it. Any and all impediments to having a clear and open heart for God to pour Love through will continue to arise, and God will continue to remove them.

You may re-experience briefly in your mind and emotions the situations that created these impediments, even with some discomfort. This is the "replay" as the removal is occurring. If this occurs, know that it is of the past, and do not be concerned. Simply pray gratitude, giving thanks for the fact that all blockages to your completely open heart are now being removed. Reading the excerpt from the Messages from God at the end of the Meditation will clarify this.

As you do the Meditation, read a paragraph, and then close your eyes and allow time to completely absorb the experience. You may want to record it on a tape and play it back to yourself.

Meditation On Dissolving Impediments To Open The Heart

Begin by taking deep breaths, sinking into your heart with all of your consciousness. With every breath in, open your heart, larger and larger and larger. As you breathe in and your heart opens, feel yourself connecting to the All of God, the great ocean of Love, vibrant and alive, vast, yet tender.

So now you have a gloriously open heart connected to the All of Love. The vast, the un-manifest. And now you feel that ocean of God's Love permeating your being and funneling through your heart. Not just your physical heart, of course, but the heart of Love that you are. With every out-breath, God pours through you to touch and love manifested life.

We are aware of ourselves now as that point where God loves through us. Be conscious of how it feels as Love pours through you. Feel how it blesses, how it kisses every cell of your body, how it illuminates every particle of Love that you are, how it resonates with the light that is in every atom, with the life that you are. How does it feel to be the very heart of God?

Breathe in, becoming the open heart, communing with the All of Love. Breathe out as Love pours through the opening that is you and God's Love comes into the world. Notice how it feels to be touched by this Love, to be its vehicle, its vessel. Allow the Love to pour through you and your mind to notice, AFTER the fact. Notice, if you can, how this Love honors the truth of who you are, your existence.

As you feel this Love pouring through you, keep expanding in your awareness of the heart that you are. Expanding until there is nothing else. No personality, no body, only the glorious opening for Love. Feel the celebration of life, exaltation, joy as that Love pours through you. Notice that there is only Love, washing through you, pouring through you, rushing through you, without discrimination. It doesn't go some places and not to others. It doesn't find some lives worthy and others not. It just pours through you. All of life manifest is being loved through us. The rushing, dancing river of living Love, pouring through the heart of God we are.

Now placing our consciousness right at that point that is the opening of our heart, the place where God's Love pours through, the window pane of our spirit – the heart – allow to rise up before this opening something that restricts the passage of this Love — something that is a belief or a part of who you think you are, something that needs the forgiveness of letting go. Allow it to rise up from within from the wisdom that God is with you. Hold it there in front of the opening that is your heart.

Now, breathing in – connect to the glorious All of the Love of God and allow that Love pouring through your heart to love that flaw, that part that needs releasing. To love it, to love it, to pour that Love upon it with passion and with tenderness, all the urgency of the river of life, reaching through to lift it up, to dissolve its hold on your heart. Love washes it tenderly until you see it dissolving, until where there was a blockage, there is only living Love. Know that anything exposed to this Love can only dissolve, its energy freed at last.

And now, breathing in, you are held within the All of God. You are held in Love so magnificent that you are filled with joy and love so tender that you are sure in every fiber of your being of God's personal support of you. You are suspended in abundance and perfection – the perfection of God's Love for you. You are resting in the ocean of God and you are filled with a clarity you have never known – the experience of how precisely God shows you your unique beauty, the truth of your creation. This glorious all-encompassing, personal yet limitless Love of God reveals to you the full capacity of your heart, so that now…

Breathing out, God's Love now flows through you completely unimpeded. The opening that is the center of your being, the great heart that you are is filled with ecstasy because now you are aware that this very same tender uplifting, deeply personal Love of God you have experienced, can pour through your heart. In this way God may reach others through the sacred opening for Love that you are. The "window-pane" of your spirit, the center of your being, your heart, is crystal clear.

Breathing in, you feel the sweet support of the All of God, reflecting to you your truest self. Breathing out, you know yourself as the clear unimpeded heart through which God now perfectly loves the world. Every person, every plant, every particle of energy – God will love them through you. And as divine Love is ever moving through you, you will be giving beyond any thought or desire to receive. Just so will you truly receive all that you give, which is now all that God gives through you, multiplied and delivered to your open and accepting heart.

Now you have the assurance that all impediments will be removed from your heart by God. So you can simply rest in this assurance – that God will do the work of Love in and through you now in each and every moment.

Commentary on Dissolving Impediments To Opening The Heart

Excerpt from *The Messages from God*
Through Yaël Powell, Circle of Light
November 24, 2002

"The impediments before your heart, any one of you, unravel like a skein of wool when the Love hits it, and unraveling, they do 'replay' themselves. They engage the projector, pull down the screen and play a movie in your mind. For, of course, this is what life in the ego really is – billions of unraveling 'movies' playing out the mind's beliefs, over and over, as the light of My Love seeks entry.

"Yet you can know, you who now begin to come to the central point consciously, that the more you stay 'out of your mind,' the fewer 'new movies' you create, and soon (sooner than you think), there won't be any 'movie reels' left to play.

"When you say, 'Yes,' to Love, you are saying that you are willing to dissolve those impediments. To let the light of My Love into the movie theatre. Thus, for you who see your lives becoming beauty, the reflection of your heart — you can know that if suddenly you are 'in the play' again, it IS the clearing out of those things cluttering up the heart space, those things that 'push the pendulum' so that it swings away from the center point. Especially if you are choosing to accept the tools given [the above Meditation], then you can positively know this is the case, and that it won't take long and you will be able to remain in the stillness of My Love, allowing Me to live every moment through you."

A LETTER FROM GOD TO HUMANITY ON CREATING A WORLD OF LOVE

Through Yaël and Doug Powell
February 25, 2003

My beloved ones, humanity, I pour this to you with My tender Love, upon streams of light, to touch your waiting hearts. With it come the keys to your remembrance. The remembrance of your beauty and of all the ways I made you in My image. And remembrance of the truth of Love, how every human heart was born in Love and every human being is a child of God. And the remembrance that your heart is our connection and that through it lives your co-creative power. Through it comes your treasure; all the gifts I give to you forever. Through it you will now remember and find yourselves awaking to the truth of Love you are.

How I love you! You are truly the greatest of all miracles. You are My own heart, alive and in embodiment, ready to expand, to ever go forth to give the Love you are. You make Love vibrant, surprising, new. Only you, beloved ones, My precious glorious children, only you can go forth in breathless anticipation and see the Love I Am with a new perspective. Have you not marveled at your wonderful curiosity? At how insatiably you go forward to meet and greet the world? And how deeply you are moved by every expansion of beauty? This is the miracle of your co-creative heart.

My Will for you, all of you, every sweet magnificent golden child of God, is a world of peace and a life of plenty. By looking at Me, you can have these things.

Your heart is the source of your power, your treasure, your identity, your life. Your heart is connected to Me forever. And through your heart you will receive your blessings, the treasures of joy and Love and ever greater abundance that I have waiting for you. Oh! It is My heart's true desire to deliver to you the very keys to heaven that you may live heaven here on Earth, yes, and everywhere you are for all eternity. All that is necessary is for you to return to your heart to find the joy in life that contains the heart's true resonance and the cornucopia of every good, which shall pour forth before you as your life and your world.

I Am a God of Love, dear ones. Forever and forever. There is nothing but Love in Me. Let your heart stir in its remembrance of the great truth, for on it rests the salvation of this precious world and your thousand years of peace that, truly, goes on forever. You have known this, somewhere deep inside. You have known that I Am Love and that all of this before you did not make sense. All the wars and illnesses, the brothers turning upon their brothers, the poverty, the pain, even ageing and death. Oh, dear ones, I have heard you as you cried out in the dark night of your soul for answers. How every single one of you has asked the question, "If God loves us, why would God create children who have cancer and whole peoples who are starving; so emaciated they already look like skeletons?" It did not seem right

258

to you. This, dear ones, was the message of your heart seeking to show you the truth. And when you have asked, "God, what is my purpose, the meaning of my life?" you have been responding to the nudging of your heart. But some, not hearing their hearts, have turned away, believing I could not be a loving parent to My children if I created such a world of horrors.

Now it is time for the truth. You are ready. And for those of you who read this and already know this, I ask you to deepen your commitment to the living of it, and to pass this on to My other precious children. For those of you who read this and find it inconceivable, I ask you to drop into a focus on your heart for a moment and just allow this to be a possibility. Then pass it on to others – that each hand, each set of eyes, each heart that comes in contact with this letter written in light may also take a moment to allow this possibility to be planted in their life.

Beloved ones, I love you. I love you with a Love as great as the very cosmos. I love you with a joy in your existence that pours forth greater in every moment. I love you as the very heart within Me. I love you, and My Love never wavers, never changes, never ever stops. I long for you to know this, to feel our sweet communion. I long to lay before you all the treasures of creation. You are Mine. Now. And Now. Forever. And nothing can ever change this. It is a fact of your existence.

I did not create this world of pain. You did. You did this when you chose to believe in good, in Love, *and* in something else, which you named the opposite of Love. Call it the moment in the Garden when you ate the fruit of good and evil. Call it the first judgment. Whatever you call it, beloved ones, it is your own creation. And you set yourselves up as being able to decide which was which and thus began this world of duality, of light *and* dark, of Love and anti-Love. But, precious humanity, I Am only Love. And living in Me, you, too, are only Love. So you had to create a false world, a pretend place where darkness could exist, because it cannot exist in that which is ever and only light, which I Am.

You have wandered in the desert of your co-creative minds ever since. For if your heart, connected to Me, knows the truth of only Love, then you had to find another way to view a dual scenario – and thus evolved the tool of your minds.

Oh, dear ones, I do not intend to go into lengthy explanations. All I come to say to you is that you are only Love. And that the more you choose to live through your heart, the more and more clearly you'll see the world as it really is. The more you will experience that true Love of God, the Love that I hold you in each and every moment.

Today you live in a world on the brink of war, a world filled with negativity and so much pain that you have to numb yourselves to survive. So you have nothing to lose by putting to the test what I now show you:

If you know that I Am only Love, then you must

know that I Am ever holding for you the world of your inheritance, the world of joyous ecstasy and glorious abundance. You know that I Am not a power you can call on for overcoming darkness, for darkness is not in Me. You know that any moment you connect with Me you connect with the Love and perfection I have always held for you and always will. I Am unchanging Love. In the truth of this Love there is no negativity.

Then what about this world of pain before you? What of the wars and rumors of wars? What of the fear and all the experiences that keep happening in your life? They are you, dreaming, beloved one. They are you lost within the million threads of possibility streaming from your decision to believe in good *and* evil. And just as you dream in the night and your dreams feel real, so it is with this world. So very real and filled with pain, it feels.

There is another way to live. It is to stand before this world of lies each morning and to choose to live in only Love. To consciously reject the illusion of the judgment that there is good and evil. To place your Will in Mine and ask that I lift you up enough that you can see the difference. The difference between the truth of Love that lives within your heart and this world of swirling negativity that is alive within your mind

And once you know that I Am Love and you are ever alive in Me, then you shall truly walk through this world in peace. When you know your home is Me and you affirm the heart, you could walk through a war-torn countryside with bombs falling all around you and know that none could touch you, and none would touch our home.

I will answer your questions. "What about the others?" your heart cries out. "What good is it if I am safe in you, God, if all around me people are in misery?" Beloved ones, the answer is this: as you clear the dream, as you return your Will to Me, as you walk within the truth of the Love we are together, then around you there becomes an aura of peace; a great ball of light comes forth as the living truth of Love you are becoming. At first it may only clear *your* life of the illusion, as your faith in Love restores you to the heaven you belong in, and as, choice-by-choice and day-by-day, you turn to Me for your identity and not to the world you have believed is outside of you. But every day that light grows – exactly as would happen if you turn on a physical light in a dark closet full of scary shapes. The light fills every space – there is no darkness left – and everything that seemed to be so menacing becomes something neutral. Something you can change by moving out the old furniture, or something that you at least know is harmless.

Thus, as you grow in your ability to stay attuned to Me, to choose the world that is your birthright as a child of God, the greater the circumference of the light that surrounds you. First it begins to light up your neighbors. Suddenly they can see that there are no terrifying things lurking in their lives; that they are free to choose to be happy, to have joy. And with every moment that you spend in communion with the truth of your heart, the greater is that light of truth around you…until you affect the neighborhood and then the town you live in, and the county, then the state in which you live. Until ultimately you will do as Jesus did: everywhere you are, people will see their truth as Love, and knowing this with all their heart they will leave their illnesses, their problems and their strife behind – simply from experiencing the power of your light as you live your life as only Love.

Then as others do the same, soon you'll walk into the world and the illusion of negativity will have to fall away. You will have "turned on the light in the theater," that which you call the world, and all who had believed life was a battle will suddenly be freed.

In your Western world, there is a passage in the Bible from he who came to show you the way to the heart's truth: "You cannot serve both God and mammon." This is exactly what it means. You cannot believe in a world of good and evil and also seek to create a life of Love. For from within the dream of duality every choice for Love contains its opposite.

Beloved ones, if this speaks to you, if something stirs within your heart (or, of course, if you cry out, "Oh, I know this!"), then you are here to show the way. Here to see My face, My Love, in every human being, no matter the part they now play within the dream of good and evil, of Love and anti-Love. You are here to build the New, to bring forth the heaven of living Love in which you are ever meant to live. Turn to Me and daily, moment by precious moment, I will show you who you are: a child of Love so beautiful that your cloak is made of stars, your heart is a living sun lighting up the darkness and revealing only light.

Give Me your Will, let Me lift you so you can see each moment the unity of Love. How all creation is My being and every part, magnificent and joyous, dances in a swirl of sweet exploding life. I will help you see beyond duality, beyond the veil within which lives the dream of separation being dreamed by My children. I Am only Love. And your heart is the key to the treasures held for you beyond time. Time – the illusory creation coming forth from "fitting into experience" a pendulum of good and bad experience.

Beloved ones, I speak to you whose hearts have known, have known deep inside that I would not create such a world as this you see before you. It can be easy to disengage, but you've lived the illusion for a long time. Thus can you assist each other in this. Assist each other in placing your attention on your hearts and using the power of Love you find there to infuse the world you want, not the world that's passing, the world of so much pain. You are co-creators. Made in My image, remember? It is true. You are made in My image and thus do you manifest the beliefs of your heart. Remember, the heart is where we are connected, so all the power, all the light, all the Love I pour to you comes directly and unfailingly to and through your heart. I Am Creator; I Am Love expanding through you.

And My covenant with you, My children, is that I shall always and forever grant your heart's desires. This is the promise given to each of you at the moment of your creation as children of the Love I Am. So if deep in your heart you are afraid, if you believe your heart is broken (pay attention to these words), if you are afraid that Love will hurt you, if you keep yourself protected, if you are waiting every moment for "the other shoe to drop," if you feel the world is hopeless, if you feel that life's not worth it, if you feel the world's about to end, be it from polluting it to death or from chaos and war, these deep "ways you feel" about your life – these are your heart's beliefs. And thus, beloved ones, *by our covenant* they shall manifest before you. For as the Love I Am comes pouring to you, whatever is held before the opening of your heart is what Love shall bring to life, shall help you co-create.

Thus you see that, if you stand before the White House with anger in your heart, with belief that nothing changes, that government is corrupt, and, worst of all, if you hold hatred there, within the temple of God that you are, then that, dear ones, is what you shall have more of.

You are the prize of the universe – the heart of God gone forth to create. There is really only Love to create with. But if you choose Love and anti-Love, you turn your face away from Love and, peering into the world you've made, you look for your identity. Oh, precious ones, don't find it there! Please wake into the truth of Love. Place your every resource with your true and glorious heart. I promise you that Love is the only power. And that, truly, it is the heart with which you shall always create what you experience, be it now, on Earth, or later, "after death." There is no progression, no good and bad, no better and best. There is only the truth of Love or the dream of separation.

If you can make this leap, you are those who bridge heaven and Earth, who begin to reclaim the paradise you never really left. But if you cannot, then please do continue on growing in your faith in Love. It is good to pray for peace, for even though it contains the belief in its opposite, for the moments you are focusing on Love you are using your co-creative consciousness to lift you ever closer to the unity of Love. It is best, however (and I use these terms because they are relevant here), it is the true way, the way that Jesus came to show you, to see only Love. To place every bit of the power of your heart upon the paradise of Love that this Earth is in truth, giving none of your energy to the illusion that I can ever create anything but Love.

Do you see? Do you see how this must be a fantasy if in Me darkness does not exist? If I Am All That Is, which I Am, then nowhere in Creation is there anything but Love. Oh, dear ones, this I promise you. You were created in Love; made as a glorious reproduction of what I Am as Creator. You thus came forth, truly, as Twin Flames, the forces of the Divine. Ocean of Love, Divine Feminine, and the great movement of My Will upon it, Divine Masculine. Born as one with two points of conscious Love, you forever exist in a grand unity of Love, sparking together to co-create more Love.

I call you home. Home to the unity of Love I Am and that you are in Me. Every thought for peace, every prayer has value, and every act of service in Love's name to another is a star in the night of this "pocket of duality." But the real service for which many of you have come is to join together, heart after heart, in the conviction of the truth of only Love and, forming a net of your great auras of light, to lift the world free of the reversal caused by humanity's belief in good and evil.

Thank you, beloved one, for reading this. Do you feel My living presence in your heart? Do you see the light behind these words, the packages of Love I now deliver? Then you are called, beloved one. Called to remember a world of only Love. Called to place this vision before you until it sinks into your heart and becomes your one desire: to return to My children their birthright. You have angels all around you. Your hands are being held, finger of light to finger of light, by the masters who go before you to pave the way. Your every affirmation of the world of Love you choose is heralded by archangels as they trumpet across the heavens, "A child of God awakes! A child of God awakes!" And choruses of beings, living stars greater than your sun, carry forth the message that the whole of Love I Am is filled with rejoicing. For every child of God who returns heals those many lives of the dreams of anti-Love that sprang forth from their creative heart. And the whole of the cosmos is glad, because a hole in My heart, caused by your facing away into "darkness," is healed. The heart of God is mended, ah, but more than this: the Love I Am goes forth again as you to create new things for us to love together.

I Am calling. You can hear Me. It won't be long now, beloved ones.

ABOUT THE AUTHORS

Yaël and Doug Powell live at Circle of Light, a spiritual center in Eureka Springs, Arkansas, that looks out over Beaver Lake and the Ozark Mountains. Both Yaël and Doug are ordained ministers, and the lovely Chapel at Circle of Light is the frequent scene of beautiful sacred weddings.

Yaël spends a good deal of her time in bed as a result of pain from a severe physical disability. Her "up-time" is spent officiating at weddings or receiving the Messages from God in meditation. Doug is an artist and skilled craftsman at pottery and woodworking. If it is windy, you'll definitely find him at his lifelong passion – sailing! Shanna Mac Lean, compiler and editor of the Messages, also lives at Circle of Light. If not at the computer, she can be found in the organic vegetable garden.

Completing the Circle of Light family are their wonderful animal companions. Christos (boy) and Angel (girl) are their two beloved Pomeranians. Ariel (Duff Duff) is a pure white cat who mostly frequents the garden. Then there is Magic Cat, who has been with Yaël for 15 years. They have a deep and very special communion. Magic Cat has been communicating messages through Yaël to assist humans to understand the Web of Life. In the future, he will have his own book, "Magic Cat Explains God!"

CIRCLE OF LIGHT ORDER FORM
SAY 'YES' TO LOVE SERIES

Please send the following:

____copies of *God Explains Soulmates* @ $11 _____($3 S&H)

____copies of *God Unveils SoulMate Love & Sacred Sexuality*
@ $19.95 _____($3.50 S&H)

____copies of *God's Guidance to LightWorkers* @ $14 _____
($3 S&H)

____copies of *God leads Humanity toward Christ Consciousness*
@ $18 _____ ($3.50 S&H)

Prices are for the USA. For more than one book, reduce the S&H
for each book by $1. For postage to other countries, please email
us first and we will find the best shipping cost.

Name:_____

Address:_____

City:_____

State:_____ Zip Code:_____

To use credit cards, please go to our web site www.circleoflight.net
OR you may fax your order with credit card to (479) 253-2880.
If it is busy, call 877-825-4448 and we will activate the fax.

Name on Card:_____

CC#:_____ Exp. Date:_____

If you would like to be on our email list and receive monthly
Messages from God, please fill out the following:

Email address:_____

Circle of Light
3969 Mundell Road, Eureka Springs, Arkansas 72631
www.circleoflight.net
connect@circleoflight.net
1-866-629-9894 Toll Free or 1-479-253-6832, 8132